When We Pray

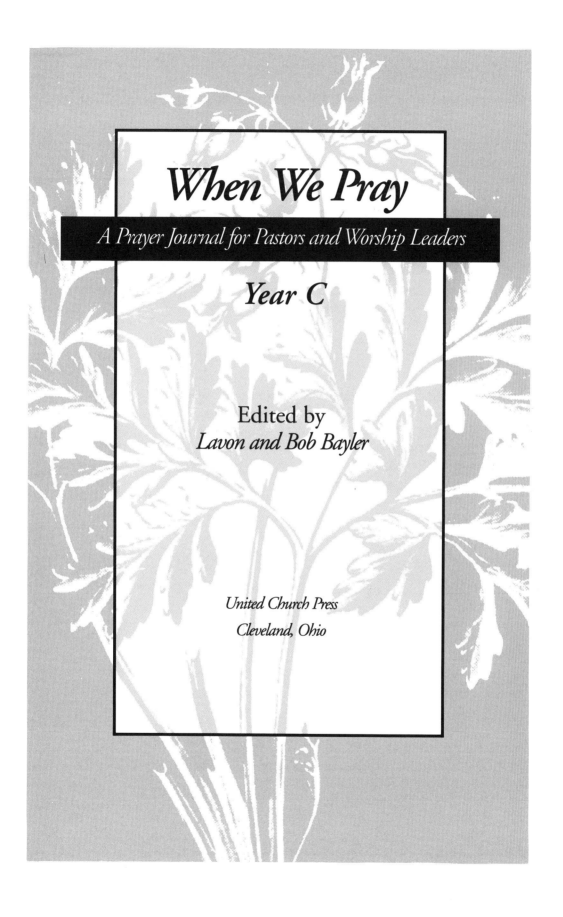

When We Pray

A Prayer Journal for Pastors and Worship Leaders

Year C

Edited by
Lavon and Bob Bayler

United Church Press
Cleveland, Ohio

United Church Press, Cleveland, Ohio 44115

Biblical quotations are from the New Revised Standard Version of the Bible, © 1989 by the Division of Christian Education of the National Council of the Churches of Christ in the U.S.A., and are used by permission

Printed in the United States of America on acid-free paper
02 01 00 99 98 97   5 4 3 2 1

Library of Congress Cataloging-in-Publication Data

Bayler, Lavon, 1933–
      When we pray : a prayer journal for pastors and worship leaders / Lavon and Bob Bayler.
          p.   cm.
      Includes index.
      ISBN 0-8298-1028-5 (alk. paper)
          1. Church year—Prayer-books and devotions—English. 2. Pastoral prayers. 3. Common lectionary (1992) I. Bayler, Bob, 1934– . II. Title.
      BV30.B39   1995
      264'.13—dc20   94-39950
                                                                                                    CIP

When We Pray: A Pray Journal for Pastors and Worship Leaders, Year A, ISBN 0-8298-1103-6
When We Pray: A Pray Journal for Pastors and Worship Leaders, Year B, ISBN 0-8298-1028-5
When We Pray: A Pray Journal for Pastors and Worship Leaders, Year C, ISBN 0-8298-1159-1

To all who have and will
give leadership
in the
Fox Valley Association
Illinois Conference
United Church of Christ

With special thanks
to the contributors to this book:

Jennifer Amy-Dressler
Eugene Birmingham
Philip Desenis
Elaine Eachus
Marvin Englesdorfer
Victor M. Frohne
Carla Grosch
Keith Haemmelmann
Julie Ruth Harley
E. Lynn Harris
Janet Hisbon
Bill Hoglund
Laura Hoglund
David McCurdy
Paul R. Meltzer
Fritz Newenhuyse
Bob Sandman
Don Schmidt
Ed Spry
David Strang
Susan Tyrrel
Art Zillgitt

Contents

Preface

Prayer is so much more than words. Sometimes there are no words for those profound occasions when we are truly attuned to the Creative Energy of the universe. God is so far beyond our most expansive thoughts that to seek to communicate through our limited understandings and verbal skills seems almost an affront. Yet words are one important channel of expression, and praying the Scriptures is one way to express our yearning for contact with the Source of our being.

The *Revised Common Lectionary* provides for us a well-ordered approach to the riches of the Hebrew and Christian texts that inform our faith systems and daily lives. Prayers that reflect the passages for each occasion in the church year can draw us into our study of them. In the pages that follow, you will find the reflections of a variety of authors whose encounter with the Scriptures is reflected in answering prayers. It is our hope that they will lead you into the texts themselves and into your own attempt to express in words your encounter with the Source of all inspiration.

Bob and I have spent all our adult lives in various forms of ministry. Writing for others has been a fairly recent venture and a very fulfilling one. For this volume, we decided to extend an invitation to colleagues ministering in the Fox Valley Association, Illinois Conference, of the United Church of Christ to join us in this enterprise. A few of them accepted the challenge. Their contributions are identified in these pages. We thank each one of them for enriching these pages with their sharing.

During year C, the Gospel of Luke is at the forefront. It is probably my favorite gospel. I find the compassion and inclusiveness of Christ, seen through the eyes of a first-century physician, very appealing. The Hebrew prophets, especially Jeremiah, are also featured during this church year. Selections from the Epistles cover much of First Corinthians, Galatians, Colossians, First and Second Timothy, and Second Thessalonians, following the pattern of semicontinuous readings.

After Pentecost, a second track is offered for the reading from the Hebrew Scriptures and the answering psalm. This alternative seeks to pair these readings with the gospel selection. The Roman church has tended to follow this design. For some of the Sundays after Pentecost, you will find an "alternate" prayer that takes note of this option. As we use the lectionary during this long period of "ordinary time," we are advised to choose one pattern rather than alternating, but the prayers in this book seem useful regardless of the worship choices we make.

Reflection pages may be used to keep a record of dates and subjects of intercessory prayer and/or to write prayers of your own. We suggest that you give attention to the scriptures for this lectionary year which were not used in this book. They are noted by an asterisk in the index. Note especially this combination of Easter Day lections: Isaiah 65:17–25, Psalm 118:1–2, 14–24, Acts 10:34–43, and Luke 24:1–12. The after-Pentecost option of "paired" passages from the Hebrew Scriptures are listed in a center column under each proper and date when no prayer based on them is provided. You may add to this book's value to you by writing prayers based on these texts, in combination with the New Testament readings for the day.

We invite you, then, to pray the Scriptures with us in your times of personal meditation. If you are tempted to use these prayers in public worship, we urge diligent preparation that brings the thoughts gathered here into the context of your particular time and setting of ministry, with attention to the needs of people in the congregation, community, and world scene. May the Spirit touch our lives as we pray.

—Lavon Bayler

The Advent Season

Reflections

First Sunday of Advent

JEREMIAH 33:14–16   1 THESSALONIANS 3:9–13
PSALM 25:1–10   LUKE 21:25–36

God of justice and righteousness, God of mercy and promise, we trust in you. Amid all that weighs us down, we lift up our souls to you. Against the treachery of these times, we cry out for your presence. You are a God of steadfast love and goodness. You are the God of our salvation. We wait for you now in these moments of silent anticipation.

Before your awesome majesty, we are aware of our finite understanding and limited faithfulness. Weighed down by worry, we do not realize our best. Distracted by enticements that compete for our attention, we forget that we are your children. Beguiled by our self-important busyness, we forget to pray. Immersed in the immediate, we miss the larger picture of your redeeming love and your coming realm. Help us, O God, to value your Word and receive your instruction.

We thank you, gracious God, for the promise of Christ's coming. Alert us to that presence we often miss, sitting next to us, stumbling down city streets, looking up to us in the trusting eyes of a little child. We are grateful for friends and family you have given us to love. Help us now to broaden the circle of our caring. Allow us to be humble communicators of all that Christ taught in word and deed. We would keep covenant, devoting ourselves to growing in love toward you and one another. Strengthen our hearts in holiness, that we may be blameless at the coming of our Savior Jesus, in whose name we pray.   *Amen.*

Second Sunday of Advent

MALACHI 3:1–4   PHILIPPIANS 1:3–11
LUKE 1:68–79   LUKE 3:1–6

By your tender mercy, Gracious God, the dawn is breaking. Your light is on the horizon, giving promise of a new day. As once you came among us in the person of Jesus, come again today, in this place. Look favorably on your people as we prepare ourselves to receive you in our midst and welcome you in our hearts.

O God, who can endure the day of your coming? Who can stand when you appear? Before you, our love is shallow and incomplete. In comparison with the straight paths you set before us, our lives are filled with crooked byways. We repent of our inattention to important matters. We confess our need for a savior to refine and purify us. May we embrace a baptism of repentance for the forgiveness of sins.

Thank you, God, for the messenger of your covenant in whom you delight. We are amazed by the good news of the gospel. Your grace is revealed to us in the compassion of Jesus Christ. Your love is renewed in us as we pray for one another and reach out to sisters and brothers in their time of need. May your name be blessed, O God, among all the peoples of the earth.

We long to find common ground on which true peace can be built, to see beyond the narrow vision of a particular culture and our finite interpretations. Raise up prophets among us who will not let us shirk our responsibilities, yet will remain humbly attuned to your righteousness. So fill us with understanding of your love that we cannot help but share it with the world.   *Amen.*

Third Sunday of Advent

ZEPHANIAH 3:14–20   PHILIPPIANS 4:4–7
ISAIAH 12:2–6   LUKE 3:7–18

We live in expectation of the day of festival, O God. You are the center of an Advent of joy. While we fear life's disasters, it is not so with you. Holy One, we pray that you will save those who stumble and gather all who are outcasts. Often we are among them. With joy we draw upon the life-giving waters of your salvation.

Hear our cries of repentance as we realize how often we have forgotten the meaning of our baptism. We deserve your judgment, for we have not produced the good fruit you intend. We have been stingy in our sharing, and half-hearted in our worship. Faith and faithfulness have not been central to all of our work and relationships.

May the washing of your healing hands, Gracious One, restore in us a spirit of gentleness. By its subtle inspiration, permit this gentleness to flow through our heads, hearts, and hands so that our lives can become clear examples of gracious hospitality. Allow the ordinary sharing of food and clothing to be the extraordinary gift of your visible presence. In the light of your gentle reception of each one of us, renew our capacity to use our abilities in ways that restore the joy of salvation.

Surely you, O God, are our salvation! We trust in your presence and will not be afraid. You are our strength as we offer songs of joy to the Holy One. Great in our midst, O God, is your peace which surpasses all understanding. It will guard our hearts and minds in Christ Jesus as we welcome your coming. *Amen.*

Fourth Sunday of Advent

MICAH 5:2–5*a*   HEBREWS 10:5–10
PSALM 80:1–7   LUKE 1:39–55

Our souls magnify you, O God, and our spirits rejoice in you. Before time began, your energy was creating out of nothing all that is. Before there was a planet earth, you were spinning off billions of stars, and one of them became our sun. Before there were people, you created for us this amazing earth and then made humankind to be stewards to care for it.

We confess, mighty God, that we have cared more for our own advantages than for a fair distribution of your resources. We do not look with favor on the lowly and the meek. Lowliness receives our pity, not honor; our leftovers, not our substance. We are quick to complain and slow to give thanks. We utter your name as an oath rather than bowing down to honor you. Our false pride leaves us empty and unsatisfied. We have not recognized our spiritual hunger or turned to you to find a relationship that fulfills our need.

Yet, O God, you pursue us. You sent Jesus to live out your will among us. Again and again, you reignite the spark of new life within and among us. In this season of anticipation, you offer us opportunities to rejoice, to find renewal, to know your favor, to share your love. Thank you, God, for the reordering of life that we can know as disciples of Jesus. When we give ourselves as an offering to you, our spirits leap for joy.

Loving God, may your promises reach to the ends of the earth, embracing all the world's hurting people. Grant us a part, we pray, in making those promises come true.

Amen.

Reflections

The Christmas Season

Reflections

Christmas Eve/Day, Proper I (A, B, C)

ISAIAH 9:2–7

PSALM 96

TITUS 2:11–14

LUKE 2:1–14 (15–20)

Establish justice and peace in all the earth, merciful God, that Christmastime can be an experience of joy. Let the heavens be glad, and let the earth rejoice; let the sea roar, and all that fills it. Let the fields exult, and everything in them. May the shepherds of the fields and the caretakers of your people rejoice in the good news of justice and the reduction of fear.

Thank you, God, for the glad tidings you bring through your servants Mary and Joseph. Your unexpected message caught them off guard. Yet, they listened and heard the Word. They took it to their hearts and nourished its gift in the womb of life.

May our celebration of your child, Jesus, awaken in us the good news that oppressive powers will be broken. Equip us for the struggle to lead your people out of the places of gloom into the locations of light. Strengthen our resolve to create livable dwellings for families who continually hear: "No room in this neighborhood for you." Stir up in us the courage to stand as witnesses for those who cannot give voice to the amazing gift of their lives. As if for vulnerable newborn infants who have no power or speech, many persons need to speak a saving word for the defenseless.

Help us to be the joyous shepherds of our day, who say to the city: "We know God's child Jesus. We have seen the Child of God. We're no longer afraid, for God's peace comes among all those who favor justice and discover peace. Glory to God in the highest, and peace be with you."

Amen.

Christmas Day, Proper II (A, B, C)

ISAIAH 62:6–12   TITUS 3:4–7
PSALM 97   LUKE 2:(1–7), 8–20

Gracious God, your glory shines with radiance on this day above all others. The light has dawned; we bask in the glow. Angels call out to us, saying, "This is the work of God, the one who loves you with a love that is beyond anything you know." Hearts eager, we rush to follow the path of the shepherds to see this new thing that you have done. A child is born . . . spirit poured into tiny, vulnerable flesh. Hands open, we receive the gift. In the eyes of the babe, we see the possibility. Word becomes flesh; spirit in-dwells body. This can happen in us, too.

For you are God, sovereign over all the earth. Righteousness and justice are the foundation of your reign. You have acted throughout history as you act now, to give life to your people, to save and redeem us. The light born in the baby Jesus is the light that began with creation and the first baby born. It is the light of your covenant with humanity, your promise to those who love you and who live in righteousness, to be our God. It is the light that gives us life.

Give us life once again. Be born in us today. Fill us with your goodness and loving-kindness. Pour out your spirit on us, that we may be your servants and your sentinels. Work in us, that we may prepare the way with joy for the coming of peace on earth. We pray this at the foot of the manger, in the glow of your radiance which shines from the face of the babe.

Amen.

Christmas Day, Proper III (A, B, C)

ISAIAH 52:7–10

PSALM 98

HEBREWS 1:1–4 (5–12)

JOHN 1:1–14

We hear good news! It echoes from the mountains and fills all the valleys with light. Listen to our joyous singing, O God! Your steadfast love and faithfulness are real to us in this holy season. How can we help but sing your praise and worship your majesty? The Word has become flesh among us! Your truth is revealed in one like us. In Jesus, we are empowered to become your children, receiving the grace embodied in the Christ, whose name we have claimed.

Wondrous God, let this season carry us beyond sentimental attraction to a wondrous event. Too often we have forgotten the prophet's message and ignored the marvelous things you have done. We take for granted your steadfast love and faithfulness. We are more likely to complain than to praise. Even the Christ becomes unacceptable to us when our comfort is threatened and our privileges questioned. We seek forgiveness for our denial of the light and truth you sent to us in Jesus.

Thank you for the Word lived among us and for the ways Christ empowers us to realize our kinship with you. The caring acts of Jesus move us to worship and to deeds of kindness. The loving witness Jesus presents to us inspires in us a desire to share good news. Help us, O God, to trust as Jesus did, to serve without pretense, and to risk without fear. May this holy season be a time when many are drawn into a saving relationship with you. May we dare to embody the good news for the sake of all who need it so much. We are listening for your direction.   *Amen.*

First Sunday after Christmas

1 SAMUEL 2:18–20, 26
PSALM 148

COLOSSIANS 3:12–17
LUKE 2:41–52

Holy One, the letdown after the holiday season has begun, and yet you have given us a gift that remains after all of the tinsel, wrapping paper, and bows have been tossed aside—Jesus Christ! Our hearts are full of thanksgiving and praise as we ponder the awesome event of your coming to us in human form. Just as generations of believers before us, we thank you for Mary and Joseph, who knew in their hearts the importance of their child. We thank you for disciples and apostles like Paul, whose sureness of who Christ was gave your people great faith. May all we say and do reflect this kind of faith: a faith that can withstand life's circumstances; a faith that can help us overcome our fears, anxieties, or losses. We pray that we, too, can know your love through the gift of your Child and the peace that can be ours through Jesus.

You are a God of compassion. Look upon those who are in need of your healing and helping power this day, whether sick or sorrowing, grieving, or bearing burdens too deep to share. May your spirit lift us all as we continue to experience how you work in and around us in all of life and even death.

Help us to lift up and celebrate what Jesus Christ has to offer: forgiveness, new life, and love, surpassing anything this world can give. We pray in Jesus' name. *Amen.*

Susan Tyrrel

Holy Name of Jesus (A, B, C)

January 1

NUMBERS 6:22–27

PSALM 8

GALATIANS 4:4–7 OR PHILIPPIANS 2:5–11

LUKE 2:15–21

The heavens are quiet, and shepherds are nowhere to be seen. The songs are stilled, and revelers have crept away. Gifts exchanged with loved ones are already losing their luster. A new calendar has replaced the old, but it looks the same as ones that have gone before.

We confess, Sovereign God, that we did not rush to the manger. We thought we would find the same old thing there. We figured that we knew the story and didn't need to experience it anew. It hasn't occurred to us to dedicate our new calendars to the holy name of Jesus. So, we are servants to old routines, not excited children and heirs of your love.

God, how majestic is your name in all the earth! Your glory fills the universe. Help us to see it. The earth is alive with plants and animals, great and small. All have their origin in you. The depths of space hold billions of suns, larger and smaller than our own. You created these specks of light we call stars. Who are we human beings that you care for us? Who are we that you crown us with glory and honor? Who are we that you took on our flesh in Jesus of Nazareth?

Holy Parent, you have given us your name and blessed us when we have done nothing good enough to warrant your attention. You have granted us favors we cannot earn, this precious gift of life we do not deserve. In awe and wonder, we offer our thanks. In joyous gratitude, we praise the holy name of Jesus. *Amen.*

New Year's Day (A, B, C)

January 1

ECCLESIASTES 3:1–13
PSALM 8

REVELATION 21:1–6*a*
MATTHEW 25:31–46

Eternal God, for whom time does not exist but in whom we live the time of our lives, you have crowned us with glory and honor, that we should be given dominion over the works of your hands. You have put all things under our feet—all plants and animals and the resources of the earth.

We schedule our time by the earth's revolutions around the sun, but it is given meaning and purpose by revolving around the Righteous One. More than by dates, life's meaning is marked by birth and death, planting and harvesting, reaching out and withdrawing, weeping and laughing, loving and hating, fighting and reconciling. You give us a sense of past and future and fill us with wonder before all your gifts.

You make all things new, which leaves us at once fearful and joyful. We are afraid of changing times but can trust your love as time moves on. We rejoice that part of your change will be the wiping away of mourning, tears, and pain.

More than all else, prepare us for the end of time, when we are judged not by the length of life but by its quality. If we can look back on feeding the hungry and thirsty, clothing and welcoming strangers, and visiting those who are sick or imprisoned, we will remember time well spent. Enable us to judge the meaning of the minutes and hours of our days now as you will judge our years, by our ministry to Jesus through our ministry to "the least" of our sisters and brothers. May our living fulfill our praying so that another year will find us ever faithful to the Christ.   *Amen.*

Second Sunday after Christmas (A, B, C)

JEREMIAH 31:7–14
PSALM 147:12–20

EPHESIANS 1:3–14
JOHN 1:(1–9), 10–18

O God, our Creator and Redeemer, you hold all life in your steadfast care. In this new year, put far from us all that weakens your good creation: human animosities, fears, ignorance, and isolating self-pity. Let your Word show us the promised renewal of creation and rebirth of human spirit.

O Christ, God's Word in our midst, you have blessed us, chosen us, and destined us in loved to be your sisters and brothers, your church. In our worship, give us a glimpse of God's mystery. In our faith community, make us examples of your forgiving love. In our serving, make us instruments of your redeeming work, that wherever you are unknown, your people may bring good news of light and life.

O Holy Spirit, you are the assurance of our inheritance as heirs of God's grace and care: Make whole all lives that are in want, raise up those who falter, console those who weep, and bring to safety those who are lost. Especially we pray for [names]. Make each one merry with the joy and comfort of this season. Feast them with the abundance of your peace, and embrace them with your wondrous love.

So may we sing your praise, O God of all our days, as we continue to celebrate the festival of our Savior's birth. Stir up in our hearts the precious gift of faith, brighten our memories of your past help, and wrap in the human form of our lives your great promises for all of life; for we ask this through Jesus Christ, who with you and the Holy Spirit lives and reigns, one God, now and forever. *Amen.*

Paul R. Meltzer

Reflections

Reflections

Epiphany and the

Season Following

Reflections

Epiphany of Jesus (A, B, C)

ISAIAH 60:1–6   EPHESIANS 3:1–12
PSALM 72:1–7, 10–14   MATTHEW 2:1–12

Holy and gracious God, giver of light and sight, arise and shine on us! By your light, help us see again who, and whose, we are. So often the shadows seem thick and our path obscure. The suffering among us and around us mystifies us; the violence in our communities stupefies us; our own resistance to change perplexes us. Brighten our vision, we pray, that we may see your hand and even your plan through it all, for we long to know that your righteous will still prevails.

Even more, we yearn for hearts warmed by the passion of your Child. Move us, like the Magi, to search fervently for your leading and rejoice greatly when we find it. May we in the church be revealed to others and to ourselves as those who feel your call—and heed it—wherever human need cries out. Move us to grieve over poverty, injustice, and oppression; move us to give of our substance and ourselves in response.

We pray for all who suffer and struggle with illness, injury, and the frailties of this life. We pray especially for those in hospitals and institutions, and those who feel alone and isolated in their struggles. May they know your presence and power with them and for them; may they feel the brightness of your rising!

May we in this congregation be ministers of your light, with minds enlightened by your truth and hearts kindled by your warmth. We pray in the name of your incarnate Child, even Jesus Christ.   *Amen.*

Epiphany of Jesus (A, B, C)

ISAIAH 60:1–6   EPHESIANS 3:1–12
PSALM 72:1–7, 10–14   MATTHEW 2:1–12

We thank you, God, for assigning the gift of grace to the apostle Paul. All of us born outside the circle of your chosen people rejoice that we, too, with the Jews, are now joint heirs of your care. We are part of the same body, one family of faith, sharing together in your promises. We are grateful that, by your grace, we now have free access to you through confidence and trust in Christ, who is the light of the world.

May we, like the Magi, follow your star. Forgive us if we put off the journey to which it calls us. You command us to rise, shine, and give you the glory, so others may be led out of life's shadowy places into the light. Teach us to sing your songs in places of science, business, politics, and education. May we reflect your light among those who are poor, hungry, sick, wealthy, or uninvolved. Let our lives mirror your love to cowardly souls, to people who have never heard your name or known your promises. Send the light of your truth among all who have given up or given in to the lusts of the world.

If saints are those through whom your light has shown and shines yet, then make saints of each of us. May the guiding light of your star radiate through the stained glass of our lives in a rainbow of hope, joy, and peace. Hear now our petitions for hurting sisters and brothers throughout the world. [Offer petitions.] We ask all this in Christ's name, who is the light of the world. Now let all your people say amen.   *Amen.*

Philip Desenis

Baptism of Jesus (First Sunday after Epiphany)

ISAIAH 43:1–7   ACTS 8:14–17
PSALM 29   LUKE 3:15–17, 21–22

Your voice, O God, calls us by name in the rushing of water and in the whispers of the Spirit. Your Word echoes a hopeful truth: "You are my beloved Child; listen to me." The voice of affirmation brings a sense of being at home in your world, O God. The voice of rushing water helps us to remember that while we were yet helpless, parents honored your name and ours in the mystery of baptism.

Thank you, Jesus, for including us in God's family through the baptism of water and the Spirit. Open our eyes and hearts to the powerful unseen life of accepting and forgiving love. By your choice, O Holy Spirit, whisper into our ears, each day the accepting word, "You are my Child, the Beloved; with you I am well pleased." Move us to believe, Holy God, that we are your children, even when you are not well pleased with our behavior or speech.

Sometimes we are like Simon of Samaria. We act as if money can buy the gifts of the Spirit. Then we wonder why the transforming power of the Spirit never comes upon us. Forgive us, dear God, when the values of the marketplace invade your sanctuary. Open our minds to the truth that our hearts are not right before you. Move us, O God, to change the intention of our hearts. Wash from them the ash of bitterness and the chains of wickedness. Come, Holy Spirit, in the rushing of water and cleanse us by the forgiving grace of Jesus Christ our Savior.   *Amen.*

Second Sunday after the Epiphany

ISAIAH 62:1–5
PSALM 36:5–10

1 CORINTHIANS 12:1–11
JOHN 2:1–11

We yearn for your presence, O God, as we gather in this sanctuary among our neighbors to open our hearts, minds, and spirits to you. Be present with us, we pray, not only in this holy place but also in every moment of all our days.

How often we seek a sign, an evidence of your presence, of your gracious care. We look for blessings, for answers to prayers, for miraculous solutions. O God, be patient with us in our anxiety. Remind us again and again of your steadfast love, which endures through all seasons, in each new day, to sustain and redeem life.

Bestow upon us the gift of your spirit, which we know through Jesus Christ. We pray for the assurance of your presence. Hear our prayers for those who are alone, for those who suffer and mourn, for those who despair and doubt, as well as for those who know and share the good news of faith.

Be present with this church and all who minister in its name. Help each of us to witness to our own Christian faith, using the gifts you have given unto us. Lead us to appreciate one another's gifts even though they differ. May gifts of healing, prophecy, tongues, and wisdom work together for the common good. Help us to proclaim our oneness with Christians throughout the world who look to you in hope for justice and peace where there is now violence and war. Give us this day renewed confidence in the miracle Jesus still proclaims to all: Christ's abiding presence with us.

In Jesus' name we pray.   *Amen.*

Third Sunday after the Epiphany

NEHEMIAH 8:1–3, 5–6, 8–10   1 CORINTHIANS 12:12–31*a*
PSALM 19   LUKE 4:14–21

Awesome God, wherever we look, your handiwork greets us. The heavens speak your wonders, and the earth resounds with praise. Your Word gives strength and purpose to your people, filling us with joy. We are amazed that you care for us, that your spirit is among us, that you call us to continue the ministry of Christ.

O God, we bow in reverence before your infinite mystery. How is it that the ruler of all worlds entrusts to us the secrets of the universe? We have heard your commandments, but we have not kept them. We have been confronted by your truth, but we turn away from it. You offer us the finest gold, yet we settle for tarnished brass. We have become so comfortable in our transgressions that we cannot detect the error of our ways. O God, do not let our sins have dominion over us. Revive our souls and turn us around.

We thank you, God, for the capacity to grow and change. We rejoice in the variety among members of Christ's body, the church. Together we can offer the combined gifts we bring to ministry. In harmony, we provide wholeness out of our diversity. We need one another. Help us to grow in respecting and valuing one another. Teach us to suffer with those who are suffering and to rejoice with those who are honored. Thank you for appointing among us apostles, prophets, teachers, healers, leaders, speakers, and miracle-workers. May all possess and give in abundance the love you so generously bestow.

May your good news reach those who are poor, unseeing, captive, and oppressed. May our lives add to the fulfillment of our prayers.   *Amen.*

Fourth Sunday after the Epiphany

JEREMIAH 1:4–10   1 CORINTHIANS 13:1–13
PSALM 71:1–6   LUKE 4:21–30

We have been leaning on you for a long time, O God. You have been a trusted
presence through most of our days. Like the air we breathe, you are near when the sun
shines or when the storm clouds gather. In you, merciful God, we have found a rock of
loving-kindness. When we have spoken thoughtless words unjustly, you have not put us
to shame. When, out of fear or low self-esteem, we have failed to reflect your intentions
in our thoughts or words, you offered reassurance: "Do not be afraid, for I am with you."
When we listen, you restore our faith and resolve.

Deliver us, faithful God, from apologetic faith. Reestablish in us the capacity to
speak the word you put in our minds. Open our eyes to see the difference between a fit of
self-serving passion and a faithful reflection of saving truth. Strengthen our talent for
distinguishing faint praise from genuine appreciation for a deed thoughtfully done and a
moment of careful listening perceptively received. Help us to believe that your spirit is
upon us, commissioning us for service in Christ's name.

Gentle Spirit, in gratitude we honor those whose quiet encouragement inspired
hope when life was frail. In quiet reflection, we remember those who did not despise our
youth, age, or town of origin, but who in faith honored who we are. In warm embrace,
we draw near to those who loved us into being and rescued us when we were in danger.
With thankfulness, we recall that faith, hope, and love are the evidence of your grace.
Today may evidence of your great love shine through all creation.   *Amen.*

Fifth Sunday after the Epiphany

ISAIAH 6:1–8(9–13)   1 CORINTHIANS 15:1–11
PSALM 138   LUKE 5:1–11

Gracious and loving God, you have revealed to us time and time again that your steadfast love endures forever. We understand this to mean that your spirit touches ours in those times and places where we are most susceptible to being loved and in those times when we are least in control. Thank you for never giving up on us, even though we so often think we can give up on you.

Grace-filled God, you fill our lives to overflowing with gifts of promise and hope. We are blessed and stewarded into such abundance that when our eyes are opened, we are amazed and overwhelmed. The responsibility of such stewarding leaves us in awe, not only of the gifts but of our own implied worth. We have seen ourselves as unworthy, but you turn us around by affirming our worth with your abundance bestowed upon us.

Searching God, you call us to share good news and our abundance with others. We understand that we are to share with them an attitude of service and an offering of self that will leave them as amazed at the giftedness of their lives as we are, and will bring them to their knees in praise and thanksgiving.

You humble us, God, before your goodness and your mercy, in ways that change who we are and how we will be in the world. We celebrate in this season of Epiphany that you have appeared to our ancestors and now have appeared also to us. In the name of Jesus.   *Amen.*

Sixth Sunday after the Epiphany

JEREMIAH 17:5–10   1 CORINTHIANS 15:12–20
PSALM 1   LUKE 6:17–26

With hunger and thirst, we come to you, living God. We hunger for your realm, where all are welcome. We thirst for the waters of salvation, which pour out your healing vitality. We would dance and laugh and leap for joy in your presence. Test our minds and search our hearts, for we trust in your mercy.

We confess that we have relied on our own ingenuity and welcomed the trappings of human progress as our security. The success of our ventures does not satisfy. We find ourselves in a wilderness of anxiety and fear. Too quickly we take the path of sinners and scoff at the righteous as if they were the pretentious ones. If only we took time to delight in your law, to meditate and pray as they do. Then, perhaps, we would find deep roots of meaning. Then we might be raised with Christ to fullness of life. Save us, we pray, from self-imposed limitations.

As we grow in the likeness of Christ, our concern shifts from ourselves to those for whom you have asked us to pray. We lift up sisters and brothers who long for your healing touch: those enmeshed in violence and despair, those caught in webs of deceit, your children dying before their time from physical hunger or spiritual poverty. We pray for people caught in traps of affluence, whose sense of values is so distorted that they cannot identify with suffering desperation. Grant us the humility and the humanity to reach out to all persons in loving concern.

O God, we rejoice that you bless us, entrust us with good news, and grant us hope in this life and beyond.   *Amen.*

Sixth Sunday after the Epiphany

JEREMIAH 17:5–10   1 CORINTHIANS 15:12–20
PSALM 1   LUKE 6:17–26

Looking around us, O God, we are painfully aware of life's challenges. We have filled our days with bustle and activity, but very little substance. We have developed a culture defined by deadlines and headlines, but noticeably lacking in community and compassion. Dreams and hopes have faded, and our vision is unclear. Our trust in human designs has misled us. Hence, we come before you seeking guidance; we offer our lives to you, requesting strength.

Since the day of creation, you, O God, have seen our great potential. You have watched and hoped with each step we have taken. Unfortunately, our choices have not always been the right ones, and the paths we have selected have not always been the best. Yet when we stumble, you stand beside us. You are with us today to uplift and to guide us. How great is your love; how enduring your patience; how wondrous your constant promise of a new and more blessed day!

Grant us, we pray, renewed vision and hope. Plant within us that burning desire to bring your message of shalom into every area of our community. Place before us opportunities to expand your embrace of our society. Equip us with Christ's compassion, for the furtherance of peace and justice throughout our world.

These are indeed challenging times, O God—days which sometimes demand more than we have to offer. But they are our times. And more importantly, they are your times. May your light of hope so permeate our spirits that we never give up, but instead continue seeking the pathway of promise that you daily lay before us, trusting in your presence each step of the way.

Amen.

Seventh Sunday after the Epiphany

GENESIS 45:3–11, 15

PSALM 37:1–11, 39–40

1 CORINTHIANS 15:35–38, 42–50

LUKE 6:27–38

We would be still before you, God of infinite mercy. We wait for your Word to deepen our sense of trust. Let your light shine into the hidden places of our lives, which need the illumination of your truth. As we reflect on the paths we have traveled, we are amazed at all the ways you have provided for us. Even in the midst of calamity, you blessed us. In the famine of our despair, you provided for us. We delight in the ways you have prepared us. We rejoice in this time of worship.

Remove, we pray, the barriers we have erected that cut us off from full communion with you. Forgive the pain we have inflicted on others, either by intent or neglect. Still our anger and fretfulness over the wrongs we have experienced. Keep us from harboring resentment. Work in us miracles of transformation that we cannot achieve by our own wills. You have asked us to pray for those who curse and abuse us. Give us strength to meet them with the power of love that rejects their actions but affirms their worth. Keep us from judging and condemning, even as we stand up for our own dignity as people created in your image and valued by you.

Thank you for claiming us as children of heaven. Let our words and actions reflect your kindness. Help us to forgive as you have forgiven us and to give the same good measure we have received. Resurrect your church, that we may be an instrument of transforming power in the building of your realm on earth, as in heaven. *Amen.*

Eighth Sunday after the Epiphany

ISAIAH 55:10–13
PSALM 92:1–4, 12–15

1 CORINTHIANS 15:51–58
LUKE 6:39–49

We give thanks and sing praises to you, O God, declaring your love and faithfulness which fill us with joyful songs.

We are delighted with the beautiful creation which surrounds us. Rains and snows water the earth. The seed which you provide sprouts in myriad ways, offering food for all living things. Out of your abundance comes the bread we eat. In your providence, good things rather than thorns shall grow.

God, your Word also benefits those to whom it is sent. We pray that it may lead us in peace and joy, that all the earth may find cause to rejoice in it. So might it be a high memorial to you, our God.

You have called us to discipleship, challenging us to build our lives firmly upon your foundations. You have called us also to examine the condition of our own spirits before we question the spirits of our brothers and sisters in Christ. Jesus has taught us that disciples are not above their teacher. Therefore, let your goodness shine through us, that we may produce good toward others.

We celebrate the promises that you have given us for ongoing life, realizing that our mortality shall yet receive immortality and our perishable nature shall put on the imperishable. We are awed at these mysteries and yet joyful that our lives can be victorious through Christ, surmounting fears and obstacles that sometimes block our way.

Continue to be our Rock, O God. Let us flourish in righteousness. Let us celebrate in your presence all the days of our life. We pray it in the spirit of Christ.   *Amen.*

Ninth Sunday after the Epiphany

1 KINGS 8:22–23, 41–43   GALATIANS 1:1–12
PSALM 96:1–9   LUKE 7:1–10

Before your holy splendor, we tremble, God of all creation. There is no one to match your glory. Honor and majesty are before you; strength and beauty are in your sanctuary.

Merciful God, sometimes we feel like foreigners in your presence. We worship regularly in the sanctuary of our minds and hearts, but often we are not truly present. We think of work, grandchildren, golf, shopping, or a vacation we want to take. Our thoughts wander everywhere but into your spirit. Yet, when we pay careful attention to your Word, we find that the foreigner who calls on your name is not a stranger in your house.

You claim us as part of your family, gathering God. You draw us into the circle of persons who honor the mystery and majesty of your welcoming sanctuary. You invite us to come near to the One who sees none of us as foreign, even when we do not feel at home with you.

God, we are grateful that your healing power is available to all. You welcome our appeals for restoration and wholeness, both for ourselves and for those we do not know personally. Your strength stimulates the energy of faith in us, empowering ministries of care among us. Motivate us to improve our skills to listen carefully to requests for presence and assistance. Move us beyond false distinctions about who is worthy of your gift of healing. Even when our diseases are not destroyed, help us, O God, not to lose hope. Grant the grace of our Sovereign Jesus Christ to sustain us on our journey toward fullness of life. Receive our prayers in the spirit of the risen one, Christ our Savior.

Amen.

Last Sunday after the Epiphany (Transfiguration Sunday)

EXODUS 34:29–35   2 CORINTHIANS 3:12–4:2
PSALM 99   LUKE 9:28–36, (37–43*a*)

Lover of justice, let your people tremble before you. How frightening it is to encounter the Creative Energy of the universe! O God, you are the Holy One whose rule extends beyond the reaches of infinity. Yet you draw near to encounter us. When we feel your touch, we are amazed. When you speak to our hearts, they expand with compassion. When we see all that you have done, our faces glow at the movement of your spirit within and among us. Transforming God, how wonderful are all your works!

O God, how seldom we come boldly into your presence, expecting and welcoming your statutes and decrees. How little we anticipate this time of worship. In our preoccupation with other things, we miss your visitation. Our hardened hearts draw a veil of resistance between ourselves and you. We try to hide our evasion of responsibility and our cunning attempts to pile up advantages for ourselves. Break through our defenses, that we might marvel in awe and wonder on the mountaintop, sensing you in ways we have never before experienced.

Prepare us this day for the crowds that need to hear good news from us. Let your disciples be empowered to carry forward the ministry of Jesus in the valleys of human suffering. May your greatness be revealed in our caring and compassion, in our healing attitudes and our reconciling deeds. Make of us a faithful, trusting congregation—not just when we are together, but as we scatter to meet the world in your great and awesome name. May all our work be ministry and all our play renewal. Thank you, Holy God, for answering our prayers.

Amen.

Reflections

Reflections

The Lenten Season

Reflections

Ash Wednesday (A, B, C)

JOEL 2:1–2, 12–17

PSALM 51:1–17

2 CORINTHIANS 5:20*b*–6:10

MATTHEW 6:1–6, 16–21

Merciful God, awaken us to a clarity of self-knowledge. Open our eyes, clear our minds, and rend our hearts, so we can experience the troubling truth that all is not well with us. The stuff of living is piled so high that we cannot see whose we are. We spend more time moving the stuff than we invest in meditating on your purposes for us. We seldom can be found in a solemn assembly called to examine our hearts.

Even now our thoughts wander to the department stores, shopping malls, and opulent exhibits where our idols are assembled. O God, draw us back and reconcile us to you. "Spare your people, and do not make your heritage a mockery, a byword among the nations." Forgive us, Holy One, according to your abundant mercy. Cleanse us from our sin of substituting stuff for love, or goods for grace. Renew in us a desire for truth in our inner being. There, in our heart of hearts, may we come clean. Wash us thoroughly from our iniquity and clear away the powerful urge to acquire more.

We realize that now is the acceptable time for changes in our lives. Restore in us the joy of your salvation, the simple delight we can find when free and at ease in your presence. Keep us from a false piety that is only for show. Rather, draw us into solitary communion with you, Gracious One, where we can rediscover life's valuable blessings. May the treasures we count most precious involve relationships, not things. May our simple prayer become: "Your will be done on earth as it is in heaven." *Amen.*

First Sunday in Lent

DEUTERONOMY 26:1–11   ROMANS 10:8*b*–13
PSALM 91:1–2, 9–16   LUKE 4:1–13

God of our ancestors, and our God, you are to us a refuge and a fortress. We have found in you a dwelling place where affliction, oppression, and endless toil lose their power to control. Your rescue and protection give us confidence. On this first Sunday in Lent, we gather in the safety of your presence to begin a season of self-examination and penitence. Hear our prayers and direct our thoughts in this hour and this season.

We admit, O God, that our trust has sometimes wavered. The words on our lips have not been your Word. Our thoughts have not centered on your will for us. We have tried to live by bread alone, choosing to focus our lives on material gain. We seek attention and power as if the measure of our worth lies in public acclaim. Our very standard of living has fostered oppression of others. We need your help to confront ourselves and realize your purpose for us.

Thank you, God, for assuring us that all who call on your name will be saved. Thank you for showing us a life of wholeness and integrity in Jesus of Nazareth. We are grateful for the witness that one does not live by bread alone, that only you are to be worshiped and served. Help us to trust, and not put you to the test. We bring to you our first fruits, offering to others what we have received. Our prayers embrace your hurting children, near and far, as we pray for those we name and for the multitudes we will never know. [Pause for persons to be named.] Hear our prayers, Gracious God. *Amen.*

Second Sunday in Lent

GENESIS 15:1–2, 17–18   PHILIPPIANS 3:17–4:1
PSALM 27   LUKE 13:31–35

You come to us, O God, as light and salvation and bid us count the stars. You are a shield to us and a stronghold, counseling us not to fear. Yet doubts and despair enter our troubled thoughts, and we are afraid. Our minds are troubled. We avert our eyes, looking down at the ground or staring into space. When we feel or believe that even our parents might abandon us, we are filled with tears and rage. When the promises of a lifetime appear to go unfulfilled, we, like Abraham, sense a deep and terrifying gloom descending on our life's journey.

Merciful God, be to us a stronghold of hope when our days seem to be constantly in the pits. Lift our eyes to see your face in the strong presence of Jesus. May the companionship of your grace in Christ transform our sense of humiliation into the energy of hope and vision. Assist us as we struggle to see through promises delayed to a life designed by persistent expectation. Let our hearts take courage and be strong as we wait for you, O God.

We are grateful, faithful God, for those unlikely people who come in your name. We are encouraged by their steady appearance, even if they don't know what to say to us. In quietness and confidence, may they and we renew our strength. Be to us a center of renewed assurance, that we may find joy in every day. Be with us as we stand firm in the affirmation: "Blessed is the one who comes in God's name."   *Amen.*

Third Sunday in Lent

ISAIAH 55:1–9   1 CORINTHIANS 10:1–13
PSALM 63:1–8   LUKE 13:1–9

O God, our God, our souls thirst for you. We have heard your invitation to come to the waters, where our thirst may be quenched, our spirits renewed, our lives restored to wholeness. In this sanctuary, we sense your power and glory, we experience your steadfast love, we are moved to joyous praise. We seek for ourselves the bread of life, which becomes a rich feast that we can share with others.

We are thankful for our spiritual ancestors who dared to leave the security they had known to journey toward the promised land. We understand their faults as well as their virtues. We identify with them in their fears, in their idolatry, in their sexual immorality. All of us are guilty of some of their sins. Sometimes we have learned from what happened to them. Often we have repeated their mistakes. We have turned away from you and complained of our lot in life. Our faith, at times, has been unequal to the tests we face.

We come to you now, weary of pretending and eager to reclaim your covenant with us. We want to forsake our wicked ways and unrighteous thoughts. Have mercy on us, O God. Take us under the shadow of your wings and bless us.

Then, O Gracious Spirit, let us be a blessing to others. Keep us from judging them from our narrow perspective. We want to perceive our brothers and sisters through the eyes of Christ, who saw their potential more than their history. Help us to bring out their best, even as we give our best in thanksgiving for your steadfast love. In Jesus' name.

Amen.

Fourth Sunday in Lent

JOSHUA 5:9–12   2 CORINTHIANS 5:16–21
PSALM 32   LUKE 15:1–3, 11*b*–32

Creator God, we use your gift of mind to deceive ourselves. We bring our
transgressions and our rage to project an image of niceness. We hide our iniquity beneath
a trivial response: "Oh, I didn't mean it." Yet, you know, O God, deep down, we did
mean it. Our unkind word, thoughtless deed, mean-spirited gossip, and petty envy are
not harmless in your sight, Holy One. Quietly, the sins of our inner being eat away our
sense of integrity. Silently, our quietness in the presence of injustice erodes the sense of
community and the safety of the neighborhood. In the presence of times of distress, let all
who are faithful offer a prayer of confession to you, healing God.

Restore in us a rightful mind. May our strength in Christ remove cynical views of
humankind. Open our hearts to affirm: "If anyone is in Christ, there is a new creation.
Everything old has passed away; see, everything has become new!" All this is from you, O
God, who reconciled us to yourself through Christ.

In this newfound freedom, O Christ, sustain us in our intention to behold the new
person in our brothers and sisters. Strengthen our resolve to receive them through faith: a
new creation. May we welcome each day as an opportunity for a renewed identity. As we
let the old one go, may we rejoice in the new day coming. Equip us to celebrate and
rejoice when the lost one is found. Let us hear you calling: Come, people of Christ,
gather in the new day of your Savior.   *Amen.*

Fifth Sunday in Lent

ISAIAH 43:16–21   PHILIPPIANS 3:4b–14
PSALM 126   JOHN 12:1–8

Gracious God, you have provided all we need. Whether we are poor or wealthy, our lives come from you. We put our trust so often in financial security. Would we pour thirty thousand dollars' worth of perfume on Jesus' head, or would we be like Judas and question such an outpouring of affection and love for the Sovereign? We believe in the wisdom of financial planners, when perhaps you are calling us to think of higher things in the allocation of our money.

Sovereign God, we confess that we put our worry over money above the belief that we can do all things through your strength. Too often we preoccupy ourselves with material worries—as valid as they may be—and do not see the beauty that is right in front of us.

For when Jesus came, you made radical claims which shake us from mundane, anxious living. As we turn to you this morning, lift us from our anxieties and fears. Help us to entrust our worries to you and know the peace which passes understanding. Free our minds from unclean thoughts and enable us to think of what is pure, true, honorable, and lovely. Do the new thing you have promised right here, right now, in our midst.

Restore us by your grace into the people we were meant to be. Help us, like Paul, to be content in all things, no matter what our circumstance. We are confident that you will form us for yourself so we might declare your praise. May we commit our days, our lives, and our souls to your Child—for it is in Christ's name we pray.   *Amen.*

Sixth Sunday in Lent (Palm Sunday)

ISAIAH 50:4–9*a*
PSALM 118:1–2, 19–29

PHILIPPIANS 2:5–11
LUKE 19:28–40

God of all of life, of laughter and tears, of misery and joy, on this day of celebration we relive Jesus' triumphal entry into Jerusalem so long ago. In our hearts we, too, cry, "Blessed is the one who comes in the name of the Sovereign!" Our children march with palm branches, reenacting the joyful procession.

But it is an ironic celebration, for we know well what lies ahead this week: the challenges, the farewell dinner, the agony of prayer and the betrayal, a trial, denials, tortures, ridicule, and death. Next week, we'll be singing hymns of resurrection glory. But that is later. Today, we seem to be hailing a victory that hasn't yet occurred. Like the fickle crowds in Jerusalem, we, too, are disappointed when you do not act as we want our ruler to act. We, too, turn away from the events in the garden and on the hill.

And yet, we are here, O Christ. We are here for the children, but not only for the children. We are here anticipating Easter, but aware of the long journey between now and then. We are here to celebrate your entry into our lives and our world—an entry that promises victory but does not bypass suffering and pain. As you rode into Jerusalem on a humble donkey, enter us anew today, Christ Jesus. Ride into [your city], down the aisles of this church, into each of our hearts. Empower us to love boldly regardless of cost, trusting that one day, this grand procession will be fully victorious at last. For it is in your living name that we pray. *Amen.*

Jennifer Amy-Dressler

Sixth Sunday in Lent (Passion Sunday)

ISAIAH 50:4–9*a*
PSALM 31:9–16

PHILIPPIANS 2:5–11
LUKE 23:1–49

Creator God, we come today to shout, sing, and pray hallelujah. And yet we have our doubts. We wonder just how much of this day we can be a part of, with our own weaknesses so near. How often we think, "Barabbas," and ignore Jesus! Our doubts cry "crucify," even if we do not say the word. Why, God, oh why must life always be such a challenge? Couldn't we have just three or four days of gain with no pain? We all want to come to supper with you, but must we go on to the garden?

Forgive us, loving God, for our denials and doubts, especially when they remain hidden inside weak and passionless hearts. We ask for your healing guidance along our path toward a faith-filled life. Help us to remember we are never alone.

Today we seek guidance for your church here at [your community]. Let our words and actions reflect the willingness of a Simon of Cyrene. Forgive us for seeking ways to minimize our efforts and maximize our stature when you give us work to do. When we are tempted to leap over Golgotha's hill to the open tomb, redirect us to walk with our Savior, Jesus Christ, even when those steps lead us into the pain-filled homes of friends or loved ones. Make your way plain before us, granting patience, strength, and courage to follow where Christ leads.

We rejoice and give thanks today for [your intentions]. May this hour sustain us through times of suffering. Lead us through Holy Week one day at a time, praying each day in the words our Savior taught us. *Amen.*

Monday of Holy Week (A, B, C)

ISAIAH 42:1–9   HEBREWS 9:11–15
PSALM 36:5–11   JOHN 12:1–11

Gracious God, you are with us at all times and in all circumstances. We give you our praise and thanksgiving for your goodness and for the in-dwelling of your Holy Spirit. In this sacred time, we pray that our awareness of salvation in Christ Jesus may be heightened. We know that in Christ we receive your new covenant of eternal life.

We bring before you our needs and concerns. We are filled with sadness. We are self-centered and short-sighted. We are insensitive to those around us who also do not know how to put their faith and trust in you. Therefore, we seek the vision of your heavenly realm. We pray for the strength of spirit to live in confidence and hope. Grant that we may be guided as individuals and as a congregation in the true light of your enlightening love.

We pray for all of your people throughout this earth. Help us to see persons who live in perilous and difficult conditions. Many struggle to survive amidst warfare. We think, as well, of those who are homeless, who have serious illness, who are hungry and destitute, who have lost hope. Deliver us all, O God, from the daily deaths we all must face. Imbue us with your holy strength. May your spirit come to all persons so that your divine righteousness, justice, and peace will be goals that we all may share.

We would honor Christ Jesus by walking in his ways, not counting the cost, but living in the joy of your love and in the service of Christ's church.

Through Christ Jesus our Savior we pray.   *Amen.*

Victor M. Frohne

Tuesday of Holy Week (A, B, C)

ISAIAH 49:1–7
PSALM 71:1–14

1 CORINTHIANS 1:18–31
JOHN 12:20–36

Merciful God, who showed your love in human form through your only child Jesus, we are so thankful for Mary, your humble servant who faced gossip, ridicule, and rejection to be obedient to you by delivering to us the greatest of all your gifts. Looking at her example, we appear selfish, self-centered, and caught up in our own problems. How can you be so patient with us when we are spinning around in circles of frustration, sometimes too dazed to choose what is right?

We are grateful, loving God, for your wisdom and understanding, mercy and grace, and especially for the gift of salvation that you made possible through your beloved child Jesus Christ. Through your power of redemption, we are saved from the pits of our self-created hells. Through your mercy, we are able to bear our burdens. Through the cross, we can face each day's trials and temptations, knowing you are with us. Through your provision, we can have hope for a brighter tomorrow. Through your unconditional love, all barriers of race, creed, color, size, shape, or gender disappear. You empower us to love those who don't love us. You strengthen our self-confidence so we can embrace equality, not feelings of superiority.

Help us to learn well the teaching from John's Gospel: "Unless a kernel of wheat falls to the ground and dies, it remains only a single seed." Help us, O God, to die to arrogance, false pride, and self-centeredness, that we may glorify you and bring others to Christ.

Amen.

Wednesday of Holy Week (A, B, C)

ISAIAH 50:4–9*a*

PSALM 70

HEBREWS 12:1–3

JOHN 13:21–32

Gracious God, we feel already the joyful triumph of Palm Sunday fading in memory. Shadows begin to curl around the edges of our vision. Betrayers of Jesus plot and plan, intent on destroying our newly blossoming hopes. The Messiah whom we receive is by others heaped in shame. Shaken, we cling to Christ, who is strong in power and determination. Jesus knows his betrayers by name and yet endures the cross for the sake of the joy to come.

God, grant us a glimpse of that coming joy, for we are weary in our own struggles and enemies rise against us. In our personal lives, we are threatened by demons of self-doubt, depression, ill health, and lack of support by those around us. In serving others, our feet are mired in past failures, lack of vision, and the plenitude of problems.

As we seek to move ahead, come to us in our poverty and need. We ask your help to lay aside every burden. Be with us as we face the enemy. Uplift us, that we may not lose heart. Feed us with the bread of life, that we may know the pioneer and perfecter of our faith. Teach us to rejoice and be glad as we learn from Christ. Go with us as we confront our betrayers. Go with us as we press on toward our goal. Our accomplishments are greater because of what we overcome. And we shall overcome. Grant us your strength in the days to come, we pray in Christ's name. *Amen.*

Julie Ruth Harley

Holy Thursday (A, B, C)

EXODUS 12:1–14
PSALM 116:1–2, 12–19

1 CORINTHIANS 11:23–26
JOHN 13:1–17, 31*b*–35

Faithful God, you kept promises with Abraham and Sarah, with Moses and the people of Israel, with Jesus and Paul. Your covenant continues with each person who loves the other. Precious in your sight, O God, are those who remember the time of Passover and those who share in the sacrament of breaking bread and drinking from the cup. By our celebrations, bring to life in us a spirit of thanksgiving for lives spared and blessed.

We remember those who suffer abuse in personal and public life. If through fear they cower in a corner of terror, then grant them courage to find strength in the poured-out life of Jesus Christ. He was abused and scorned, brought low by those who took delight in crowns of thorns. Yet by his trust in your promise, he rose above the pain and the shame. Support all those who struggle to find new life, merciful God. Even as we taste the bitterness of life, grant us the power to claim the worth of our own life and journey toward wholeness. Free us to forgive even when we cannot forget.

Come, dear Jesus, wash our hands and our feet. Cleanse our hands, that we may gently touch the wounds of our own lives and others. Through the touch, may we experience your healing power. Wash our feet, merciful servant Jesus, that we may be willing pilgrims on the serving journey of life. As we touch and travel in your name, Compassionate One, may we be open to your presence when breaking bread and drinking from the cup. Let the people say amen. *Amen.*

Good Friday (A, B, C)

ISAIAH 52:13–53:12   HEBREWS 4:14–16; 5:7–9
PSALM 22:1–18   JOHN 18:1–19:42

O day of deepest suffering. Our Savior, the Messiah who we thought would change the world, hangs dead on a cross. Despised, ridiculed, tortured, dead. On a cross . . . the ultimate demeaning act.

Yet with what dignity Jesus bore his suffering! He answered Pilate calmly, with the assurance of one who knows himself and the truth about his life: "For this I was born, and for this I came into the world, to testify to the truth." Surely he was empowered by the Holy Spirit. Can we calmly speak the truth in the face of closed ears, hardened hearts, and the possibility of losing everything? Do we suffer with dignity, accepting events that threaten to make or break our lives?

Each one of us can be empowered by the Holy Spirit to speak truth and bear insult and injury with dignity. We can do it when we are rooted in the love of God, enlivened by the Spirit, and embraced in the bleeding hands of Jesus. We can do it, because Jesus did it before us. We can do it, because God wills healing, hope, courage, strength, and love, all in God's time. We need merely ask for it and wait.

Today, we look at the broken body of Jesus on the cross, and we see in that beautiful form our own brokenness. We see the parts of us that we bear with suffering, and we commend ourselves to God. God, take this broken body, mind, and soul, and make me into what you want me to be. Let the old die to make way for the birth of the new come Easter morning.

Amen.

Saturday of Holy Week (A, B, C)

JOB 14:1–14

PSALM 31:1–4, 15–16

1 PETER 4:1–8

MATTHEW 27:57–66

The tomb has been made secure. The one whose life helped us to understand your love, O God, has died. As we enter into the story, we are desolate. It is sins like ours that put Jesus on the cross. We are the ones who want to be exclusive. We excuse our favorite sins while pointing fingers at lawlessness, licentiousness, and idolatry—in others.

On this last day of Lent, we stand under judgment. We see ourselves through the eyes of the one who hung on a cross. There is compassion and longing there—a desire that we might respond. Christ bids us love one another, for love covers a multitude of sins. O God, let your face shine on your servants. Hear us, rescue us, save us in your steadfast love. Draw us to live in the Spirit.

We have learned to look forward in hope, because we know the rest of the story. Our lives are filled with anticipation, for we have seen life come from death. We have experienced our own rebirth. Thank you, God, for the continuing assurance of your guidance and help. In your love, we live no more by human desires but by your will.

Our prayers for ourselves extend to include those who, like Job, are caught in despair. Be with all who feel alone and forgotten, seeing death as a tragic end. That feeling is not foreign to us, but we have come to know that life in your steadfast love has meaning. Grant us the courage and strength to share the good news that is breaking forth to transform your people. In Jesus' name. *Amen.*

Reflections

The Easter Season

Reflections

Easter Vigil

GENESIS 7:1–5, 11–18; 9:8–13
PSALM 46, PSALM 114

EXODUS 14:10–31
ROMANS 6:3–11

In these shadowy hours, O God, we await the coming of light and morning—not just any of the many new days which come to us out of your providence, but a new Easter Day overflowing with hope, joy, and a freshness as when bathed in clean water.

Noah, too, awaited such a time as this. For forty days he endured the rains and flood by which you cleansed and purified all that you had made. Sovereign God, we thank you for your faithfulness and for your rainbow promise of a new covenant which brings light and newness of life out of chaos and desolation.

We remember how Moses and the Israelites went through waters you parted and emerged into freedom and new life. We remember how Moses said to the people in their fear, "Stand firm: see the deliverance that God will accomplish!" Will you accomplish the same with us as we move through this vigil?

Holy and faithful God, what new thing will you do to us and through us, who, by our baptism into Christ, are also baptized into Christ's death? As the apostle Paul affirmed, united with Christ in death, we will certainly be united in a resurrection like Christ's.

O God, we believe; help us in our unbelief. You are our God, our refuge and strength. We will not fear, even though the waters roar and foam. As the Easter dawn comes, we believe we will see the great things you have done! All praise and glory be to you through our risen Savior, Jesus Christ, and through the lives we live by faith.   *Amen.*

Art Zillgitt

Easter Day

ACTS 10:34–43

PSALM 118:1–2, 14–24

1 CORINTHIANS 15:19–26

JOHN 20:1–18

Amid all the splendor of this day, Creator God, we confess our joy and our confusion. We have spent this week in the pain and pathos of Jesus' final days in Jerusalem. And now, like Mary Magdalene, we approach the tomb and find the stone is rolled away. We are humbled, for we know how unworthy we have been. We have fallen away from Jesus in his great passion. Yet it slowly dawns on us that the empty tomb is for us, and we feel the tears of undeserved joy. We are awed by the power and potential of your love. Our heads swim with the glory of your gift to us.

We thank you, loving God, for the good news of this morning which shows no partiality. We are grateful that the gift of new life is for all who hear and respond. Because Christ conquered death, it no longer limits and defines us. Every day can be Easter as we put aside old hatreds, violence, greed, selfish power and desires. As the risen Christ calls our names, we rise to lives of justice, humility, and expectancy.

Equip us, God of all nations, to tell the good news. Let our actions bring healing to sisters and brothers in their pain, hunger, loneliness, and despair. Keep us immersed in the good news so we may teach our children your ways of new life and peace. Bring that good news to countries where warring factions spill blood all over the land. Bring that good news to leaders of nations as they posture for prominence. Christ is risen! This good news is too good to be kept to ourselves. *Amen.*

Easter Evening (A, B, C)

ISAIAH 25:6–9   1 CORINTHIANS 5:6*b*–8

PSALM 114   LUKE 24:13–49

God of unexpected joy, thank you for the times when eyes are opened and understanding dawns. We are grateful for hearts warmed by your Word made flesh. On this day, we walk with Jesus and feast with our Savior and friend. Hope is reborn among us. We have good news to share.

We rejoice that you journey with us through this earthly pilgrimage. You see our doubts and lead us to renewed faith. You sense our fears and help us to trust. You observe our sins and invite us to confess them. Hear us now as we recall the ways we have distanced ourselves from you, from people who are different from us, and even from those who have been close to us. Listen to our silent confession. [Pause as silent confessions are offered.]

We ask your special blessing for all whom we privately name, praying that they may receive from you the gifts they most need. [Pause as names are silently offered.] Show us how to be reconcilers. May our children and their children and generations yet unborn receive healing, peace, and genuine love. May our lives be devoted to the realization of this prayer.

Make us now an Easter people, alive in the realization of your presence with us, reflecting a transforming gladness in all we do. May we know your salvation, not so much as a past occurrence but more as a daily joy. Every day you help us to grow and thus lead us to a new sense of wholeness. This we offer to the strangers we meet, knowing that the hospitality we offer is a way of welcoming the Christ, in whose name we pray.   *Amen.*

Second Sunday of Easter

ACTS 5:27–32

PSALM 118:14–29 OR PSALM 150

REVELATION 1:4–8

JOHN 20:19–31

God of our beginnings and our endings, Alpha and Omega of the whole universe, we have come in awe to continue our celebration of Easter. You have spoken to us your word of peace, even when we locked you out of our lives. Your voice echoes in our consciousness, even when we rebel against you. When the turmoil of our lives creates a fog through which we cannot see, your love reaches out to us. And so you abide among us now, triumphant over death, even the death of our spirits. You take us by the hand to lift us up.

Thank you, God, for calling your church to repentance. We confess that we have not allowed Christ to rule among us. We have not accepted the freedom that comes with obedience. Instead, we have tried to create our own version of freedom and thus become slaves to the world's appetites. Turn us around, gracious God, to follow in your way instead of choosing human whims.

O God, your forgiveness is real. In spite of our mistakes, you greet us. In the face of our doubts, you welcome us. Amid our faithlessness, you pour out your Holy Spirit to enliven and equip us. You send us out to teach and witness to what is beyond our knowing. You give us trust, even when we do not understand, and hope when the way is not clear. The grace and peace of Christ take root in our lives. The old compulsions and need to control are weeded out. We become your realm, the place of your dominion, the joyous company of your serving people. All glory be to you, forever and ever.   *Amen.*

Third Sunday of Easter

ACTS 9:1–6 (7–20)
PSALM 30

REVELATIONS 5:11–14
JOHN 21:1–19

Mighty and merciful God, you ask us, "Do you love me?" We hesitate. We fear the cost of loving you. We wonder if we have what it takes to be a true follower. We balk at giving up what we know for a future fraught with uncertainty, a future that may lead us to places we do not want to go.

You ask us again, "Do you love me?" Deep within, we know that you have called us by name and that we are your chosen instruments. We want to respond, to say yes with all our hearts, but fear gets in the way.

Finally, you ask us a third time, "Do you love me?" And we know that this time we cannot say no. We let go of fear and leave trepidation in the dust. We say yes with confidence, the confidence we get from your persistence in asking us. You have deemed us to be worthy to be your servants, partners in your work.

Loving God, give us the power to say yes every time you ask. Forgive us when we hesitate, and help us to let go of fear. Give us the courage of Saul, whose "yes" to you on the road to Damascus turned his life upside-down, and changed his name and the world as we know it. Help us to embrace with joy whatever path you set before us. For we know that the path you place before us is the path that leads to wholeness, for us and for the world.

All blessing and honor be yours, now and forever.   *Amen.*

Carla Grosch

Third Sunday of Easter

ACTS 9:1–6, (7–20)

REVELATION 5:11–14

PSALM 30

JOHN 21:1–19

Today God tastes the air and feels its songs,

inhaling the thoughts of yesterday and the fantasies of tomorrow.

Are we, God's children, too old to celebrate our dreams?

Let us spin our dreams to God.

Someday soon we will celebrate life every day. We will send up balloons in church.

But we would like to do it now, with our risen Savior.

We would paint gravestones as bright as the sun.

Let us glimpse the face of God in our patient parents and use the eyes of friends as mirrors.

Then we can bounce through the mountains on beach balls

and write our Christian names in the sunset.

Aspire to play in the park with children. Become as free as that person called Jesus the Christ.

We will airlift food and life to the starving and have sensors on souls as sharp as radar.

God invites us to love people simply because they are people.

Let switchblades become tubes of fingerpaint.

Color the world with rainbows of love.

In this post-Easter season, let us slow down and wait for God.

We will laugh with the falling spring leaves and dance in the drifting summer snow.

We will baptize our babies with love before birth.

We will celebrate Easter with angels and hang Christmas banners from the moon.

Yes, someday soon, people will live with such joy.

Let us plan to start right now.

Right now, Jesus, right now.   *Amen.*

Fourth Sunday of Easter (A, B, C)

ACTS 9:36–43

PSALM 23

REVELATION 7:9–17

JOHN 10:22–30

Salvation belongs to you, O God; we simply say amen. Our shepherd, Jesus Christ, guides us in times when tears need to be wiped from our eyes. We know your voice and hear your word: "Come, all who are weighed down by the burdens of life and I will give you rest." All of us need to rest in the green pastures of your presence, Lamb of God, for our souls' restoration. We walk through shadowed alleys of our cities and find no restorative power there. We walk through avenues of affluence only to find despair and meaninglessness. There is death all around us and violence in every alley. Be with us, God of our salvation, as we seek to follow the right path for your name's sake.

Prepare us to devote our lives to good works and acts of charity. Open our eyes to opportunity where mercy can provide someone with life without the fear of dying. Encourage us to take persons by the hand to lift them up to a table you have prepared for all your family. As we gather in the light of Easter, open our hearts to the possibility of being a resurrected community. Allow us to remember the successes and the failures of our church's history. Yet encourage us to belong to a new story which welcomes the stranger to your table. In the presence of bread and wine, the mystery of your body calls us to engage in honest conversations that open the heart and the mind to the family of God. Let members of Christ's family say amen. *Amen.*

Fifth Sunday of Easter

ACTS 11:1–18

PSALM 148

REVELATION 21:1–6

JOHN 13:31–35

We praise you, O God of all creation. We join with sun and moon and stars to proclaim your majesty. With all the creatures of the earth, we celebrate your goodness. You have given us the gift of awareness as we observe and appreciate and give thanks. How wonderful are all the blessings you have poured out for us!

Yet we are not satisfied with what we have. We want more, and we want to rearrange the order of all things so we can be first. We label brothers and sisters as less worthy than we. Some things we consider common and unclean. We make distinctions between people and things, pretending that our way is the only one that merits your approval. We refuse to see the gifts of the Spirit in people whose beliefs are different from our own. O God, we need Peter's vision, lest we hinder your redemptive work among us.

Thank you, God, for repentance that leads to life. You create among us a new heaven and a new earth. Daily you lead us toward holiness as you dwell with us. We rejoice that you wipe away tears, support us in our mourning and crying and pain, and bring us beyond death to new life.

Gracious One, we would offer water to the thirsty in your name. We seek to love the unloved, to feed the hungry, to reassure the fearful, to comfort the afflicted, to listen to the stories people want to tell. Grant us empathy for our mutual ministry in Christ's name. Teach us to love as we have been loved, that we might take our place as disciples of Jesus.   *Amen.*

Sixth Sunday of Easter

ACTS 16:9–15
PSALM 67

REVELATION 21:10, 22–22:5
JOHN 14:23–29 OR JOHN 5:1–9

With the psalmist and the homemaker, with the prophet and the service-station attendant, we praise you, God! We join with people in all times and places to offer our praise and thanksgiving to you who waits with us for healing and peace and for the end of our long nights of violence and hopelessness.

We praise you, O God, for your peace which can come to us when hearts are troubled and fear is dominant. When grief's sharp edge wounds us, when we lack a 3:00 A.M. courage, when dysfunctional relationships cause us to question our self-worth, when the heart has gone out of our passion for life, O God, leave your peace with us.

We praise you, God, for persistence and patience when we are like the one by the poolside waiting to be renewed. Grant us the willingness to be available to the places where renewal can take place. Move us toward places of worship and spiritual discipline. Grant us community and helpful hearts that will lift us beyond the troubled waters of our lives.

We praise you, God, for the Lydias, who have open hearts that listen eagerly to the needs within their spirits. We celebrate visionaries such as Paul, who with sensitivity of heart and spirit hear the cries for help that stretch both compassion and the good news.

Praise to you, O God, for creating us as people who make choices and decisions that can lead us into healing, peaceful, and concerned ways of life. We close our prayer with the appeal of the one from Macedonia, "Come over and help us!"

In the peace and healing of the Christ.   *Amen.*

Ascension of Jesus (A,B,C)

(may be used on Seventh Sunday of Easter)

ACTS 1:16–34
PSALM 47 OR PSALM 110

EPHESIANS 1:15–23
LUKE 24:44–53

On this day filled with wonder and hope, we gather, O God, to praise you. Hear our songs of deep joy as we marvel before the revelations of your Word. You have made yourself known to us through the law and the prophets. But, even more, we have experienced your love in Jesus of Nazareth. By your power, Christ was raised from the dead and become head over all things for the church. We gaze together into the heavens, anticipating a blessing and praying for Christ's transforming presence in our midst.

How easy it is to forget the invitation to be saints in your realm! As we seek to build our own little empires, we deny our baptism through inattention to your Word and neglect of our prayers. With closed minds and unforgiving attitudes, we forfeit the baptism of the Spirit and the power of a vital faith. Raise us up from the ruts of our lives that become our graves, that we might be lifted up with Christ to new life.

Thank you for your promise of enlightened hearts and spiritual empowerment. You open our minds to learn from the Scriptures, our hearts to care for your people, our lips to proclaim your good news of repentance and forgiveness. How rich are all your gifts for those who are willing to receive them!

Bless us, O God, that we might be a blessing to others. Empower our witness that others might meet Christ through our ministry. May love increase among all your saints as we pray for one another, offer encouragement, and serve your people with joy and abounding hope.

Amen.

Seventh Sunday of Easter

ACTS 16:16–34
PSALM 97

REVELATION 22:12–14, 16–17, 20–21
JOHN 17:20–26

By your gracious invitation, O God, we come to this place of prayer. Here your righteousness and justice are proclaimed, the faithful find a safe refuge, and all who thirst are offered the water of life. Let the earth rejoice; let the coastlands be glad. You are Alpha and Omega, the first and the last, the beginning and the end. You reign over all worlds, through all time and space. We rejoice and give thanks that you know us and welcome us.

We confess that we have not always responded with joy to your summons. Many other interests beckon us. They become more important to us than listening for your voice. You ask us to seek the common good, but sometimes the quest for unity seems to threaten our hope for gain. We are afraid amid life's storms when our certainties are shaken and our routines challenged. Save us, O God, for the community you intend.

Thank you for the witness of Paul and Silas, extending the ministry of Jesus to new places. We admire their courage in freeing an enslaved and tormented woman, their compassion that led them beyond concern for their own safety, their songs and prayers in prison. What joy they knew, serving in Christ's name! How deeply their faith influenced others!

We want to be like them. We want to trust you as they did. We long to serve as faithfully in our times as they did in theirs. In a world that does not know you, we aspire to a unity among ourselves that will empower our ministry in Jesus' name. Let your love shine through us, we pray.   *Amen.*

Reflections

Reflections

Pentecost and the

Season Following

Reflections

Day of Pentecost

ACTS 2:1–21   ROMANS 8:14–17
PSALM 104:24–34, 35*b*   JOHN 14:8–17, (25–27)

O Holy Spirit, who brought all creation into being and filled this world with good things, renew the face of the earth. Make us a new creation in our baptism.

Come, Holy Wisdom. Visit the hearts of your faithful people. Kindle in your church the fire of your love. Strengthen us by your power, illumine us by your splendor, fill us with your grace, that we may go forward by your aid. Give to your people a right faith, perfect love, and true humility. Grant that there may be in each of us simple affection, brave patience, persevering obedience, a pure mind, a right and clean heart, a good will, a holy conscience, and spiritual strength.

Speak, Holy Comforter, to every need in words and ways that each can understand. Turn the confusion of humanity's selfish deeds into the clear intentions of divine love, justice, and mercy. Bring wars to an end. Give shelter to refugees and the homeless. Nourish the hungry with both food and hope. Bear up the troubled and heal the sick. Remember those whom we remember, especially [names]. But remember also those whom we forget. Strengthen all by your might and uphold them by your changelessness, for you are our protector and defense.

So, Holy Spirit, blow away the gloomy clouds of our fears and breathe into us new life, new hope. As you came upon the apostles like fire, distributing gifts, come upon us, that we may be found constant in faith and fruitful in all works.

All this we pray to the honor and praise of the Creator, through the Christ, in the same Holy Spirit, one God, in glory everlasting.   *Amen.*

Day of Pentecost
Alternate

GENESIS 11:1–9
PSALM 104:24–34, 35*b*

ACTS 2:1–21
JOHN 14:8–17 (25–27)

O God, how manifold are your works! In wisdom you have made them all; the earth is full of your creatures. You open your hand, and our lives are filled with good things. You hide your face, and we are dismayed. We are fearful before you when we comprehend your majesty and power. Yet we are moved to sing your praise, more from awe and wonder than from fear.

But our motives are mixed. You know that well, God. You see when our worship turns from adoration to manipulation. You observe us trying to take your place, building towers of self-importance, enforcing our own will rather than seeking yours. We want certainties, and you give us challenges. We seek security, and you call us to risk-taking obedience. We focus on our own agendas, but you call us to extend your love to all the world.

Thank you for your patience with us, God. Thank you for adopting us as your very own. You have made us heirs with Christ of your own Spirit. You turn our suffering into opportunities. You make our questions an occasion for growth. The challenges we face open us to new depths of faithfulness.

Show us more of yourself, God. Let us see the tongues of fire and feel the Spirit's breath. Let the winds of your transforming presence sweep through us here in a new Pentecost. Meet each one of us in our unique identities, speaking our language in unmistakable tones. Let all the world hear you and turn away from slavery to fear. Enable us to know your truth and keep your commandments. May your peace abide with us.

Amen.

Trinity Sunday (First Sunday after Pentecost)

PROVERBS 8:1–4, 22–31   ROMANS 5:1–15
PSALM 8   JOHN 16:12–15

Triune God, how majestic is your name in all the earth! All our attempts to describe you are but partial glimpses of your glory. Your creation speaks to us of realities beyond the limits of our understanding. How vast is the reach of your infinity! How amazing the intricacy of a single cell! Your wisdom has no limits and your love no restraints.

How could we doubt you, even though we suffer? How can we deny you when there is so much evidence of your care? How can we take lightly the stewardship you have given us over an amazing ecosystem of plants and animals, majestic mountains and fertile plants, pure water and unpolluted skies? Wisdom calls us to take a stand that future generations may continue to know your bounty.

O God, we are amazed and grateful that you continue to delight in us, despite our failures. You care for us even when we do not acknowledge you. You stretch the boundaries of our prejudices and extend the limits of our endurance, developing our character and producing hope. We thank you for the hope that is in us. We rejoice in our shared hopes for a better world in which life is fulfilling for all.

Guide us, O God, into your truth. Deepen our faith and trust. Fill us with your peace. We ask this not just for ourselves but that we might serve with greater effectiveness among your people. Grant us the humility to learn from one another and the discernment to know when to speak and when to listen. May we delight in one another as you take delight in each one of us. May your grace be known to a hurting world through us.   *Amen.*

Proper 3

Sunday between May 24 and May 28 (if after Trinity Sunday)

ISAIAH 55:10–13

PSALM 92:1–4, 12–15

1 CORINTHIANS 15:51–58

LUKE 6:39–49

Dearest God, we come to you, praising you for your loving-kindness and for your faithfulness. We know that you are powerful and that your purposes shall be accomplished. We know that you enable the righteous to flourish. We know that through Christ you give us the victory over sinfulness. Help us, we ask, to resist any temptation to wrongdoing. Though circumstances may rock our boat from time to time, help us to remain steadfast, trusting in you and laboring for you.

We give you thanks for the resurrection, for the raising up of Christ and the conquering of destructiveness and death. Help us, we pray, to live now as resurrection people. Let us experience Christ's spirit living in us and raising us up, transforming us into the likeness of Jesus. Christ's living, transforming presence can change our personalities, can change us into an image of heaven. This resurrection of the spirit enables in us a fullness of life, a heightened capacity, an excelling. Fill us with it now.

Help us, dear God, to experience Christ's continued presence and activity. We ask that instead of being a trickle of living water we be like a fully flowing steam, gushing into a great river of goodness and righteousness. Allow so much to come forth from us that we can do much and produce good fruit.

Enable us also, we ask, to feel the gladness and joy that you give through your works and help us to keep on praising. But especially, we pray, help us to rise up to a new life, filled with your spirit. In Jesus' name, we ask.   *Amen.*

Proper 4

Sunday between May 29 and June 4 (if after Trinity Sunday)

1 KINGS 18:20–39   GALATIANS 1:1–12
PSALM 96   LUKE 7:1–10

Holy God, ruler of all worlds, righteous judge, how feeble is our faith! The heavens are glad, and all of nature rejoices in this season of growth. The trees sing for joy, yet we plod along in our perversions of the gospel, picking up idols along the way. We scarcely notice the substitution, for still we say, "Great is our God and greatly to be praised!" But our actions do not honor you, and our offerings are not worthy of your notice.

We tremble when we consider who you are. Far beyond the worldview of ancient prophets, your creative activity continues. Far beyond the reach of all scientific knowledge, your energy embraces unknown galaxies. In the tiniest nuances of matter, your order and design are apparent. We marvel at our own makeup—all the systems within us that work together beyond our conscious awareness. How can we dare to utter your name?

We dare to address you in the name of Jesus. We aspire to faith as trusting as that of the centurion, an outsider, who was confident of your mercy and power, revealed in Jesus. We covet the risk-taking certainty of Elijah, who challenged false allegiances of his day. Send your fire, O God, to energize our witness and empower our service.

Thank you, God, for helping us integrate all the pieces of ourselves into a wholeness and integrity that are able to reach out to others. Help us, on our journey of discovery, to listen, to care, to pass on your good gifts. May we give witness in our daily lives that you, indeed, are God.   *Amen.*

Proper 4

Alternate

Sunday between May 29 and June 4 (if after Trinity Sunday)

1 KINGS 8:22–23, 41–43   GALATIANS 1:1–12

PSALM 96:1–9   LUKE 7:1–10

O God, our God, covenant keeper, steadfast lover, hear the melodies of our hearts and minds as we strive to praise you with a new song this day! Like wise Solomon of old, we want to stretch our hands out to your heavens and say, "There is no God like you!"

It is not always easy to sing a new song, O God. Forgive each of us as so often we seem to be droning the same old tune of selfishness, unable or unwilling to open our lives to the risks of faith. Rather than risk greatness through servanthood, it has been far easier to offer solos and soliloquies to old idols. Forgive us when we've been choirs of complacency, content to live within the narrow boundaries we've set for ourselves. Challenge us to move beyond what is merely comfortable. Say the word, O God, and let healing occur. Even as you forgive us, enable us to reach out to others, that all might be set free by the truth of your saving grace through Jesus Christ!

Hear our prayers for strangers who are not yet friends, for visitors to this church and community, for anyone and everyone who somehow feels different from the rest of us. Remind us of moments when we have felt like foreigners, alone and uncertain. Help us to accept others, recognizing them as equals, welcoming them sincerely: neither smothering them nor squelching their individuality, traditions, and uniqueness.

Thank you, God, as we remember sacrifices made and battles fought to uphold gifts of diversity. Fill us with Christ's gentle courage, strong compassion, and healing touch as we reengage the world, strengthened and emboldened through this service of worship. In Christ's name we pray.   *Amen.*

Proper 5

Sunday between June 5 and June 11 (if after Trinity Sunday)

1 KINGS 17:8–16   GALATIANS 1:11–24

PSALM 146   LUKE 7:11–17

Sometimes, O God, we get carried away in destructive zeal for our particular interpretation of the gospel. Our eyes and our minds become blinded to the possibility that our perspective is driven by the demon of being right. Our limited understanding allows little freedom to our brothers and sisters to perceive Christ through the lenses of their own faith. How easily our judgments alienate, rather than drawing us all into your truth! Forgive us, O God, when we unthinkingly insist that others repeat verbatim the affirmations of faith that we proclaim.

Sensitize us, we pray, to the spirit of Jesus, which was open to the compassion of friends. Our Savior perceived in their heart of hearts a desire for the healing of a highly valued servant. Grant us the same capacity, O Christ, to move beyond the rightness of dogma to a righteousness of a healing heart. There in the innermost sanctuary of human life, help us to recover a healthy attitude of faith and faithfulness.

Out of our newfound generosity of spirit, move us to speak a kind word to and for a worried neighbor. With a new energy of spirit, motivate us to participate in constructive activities which build community in our congregation and beyond. Through a new sense of fellowship with others, awaken us all to a common hope in our Creator. Continue to watch over the stranger, the orphan, the widow, the homeless, and the sorrowing people of God. We are all children of your grace. In all times and places where life is delicate and costly, help us, O compassionate Savior, to find the healing truth of faith.

Amen.

Proper 5

Alternate

Sunday between June 5 and June 11 (if after Trinity Sunday)

1 KINGS 17:17–24   GALATIANS 1:11–24
PSALM 30   LUKE 7:11–17

Mighty and compassionate God, we stand in awe of your life-giving power, and we are thankful. By your power we live, we are sustained, and we are healed. Still, we cannot deny our mixed feelings, and even our fear, about that same power. When illness strikes or calamity threatens, we meet our old worry that what has been given will be taken away. Like the woman of Zarephath, we dread that our maker will become our slayer, that our old sins will be visited upon us or even those we love, that your anger will burn far longer than the psalmist's moment.

We know of your mercy and compassion, yet trust still comes hard for us. And so we plead: Call us out from the confining coffin of our fears! Bid us arise in trust and hope, in the certainty that you will our good. Help us to behold you as Jesus did and in the light of his compassion. Drive out the deep shadows in us that imagine such shadows in you.

We thank you for the true miracles of forgiveness and conversion, for changed hearts and redirected lives. Free us, we ask, to sing your praise and thank you boldly, that word of your loving power may spread among us and around us.

We pray this day for all who wait and hope for your healing, for assurance of your favor, for your strength in their lives. May we all be Christ's ministers, comforting as we have received comfort and strengthening as we have been strengthened. Inspire us, we ask, with trust and renewed hope in your power. We pray in Jesus' name. *Amen.*

Proper 6

Sunday between June 12 and June 18 (if after Trinity Sunday)

1 KINGS 21:1–10, 15–21*a*　　　　　　　　　　　　　　　GALATIANS 2:15–21

PSALM 5:1–8　　　　　　　　　　　　　　　　　　　　　LUKE 7:36–8:3

Gracious God, who in Christ has given us a glorious inheritance, thank you for the abundance of your steadfast love. We bow down toward your holy temple in awe. Who are we to approach your majesty with our petitions? Yet, we dare to do so because Jesus ate with sinners and welcomed those without credentials.

We know we are sinners. We may not misuse power as King Ahab did, or plot the destruction of those who are in our way as did Jezebel. But our self-conceit is at times similar, and the focus of our concern is no less selfish. We sell ourselves in pursuits that deny your purposes. Sometimes we are boastful and sometimes deceitful. Some days we cannot even be honest with ourselves. Our works cannot save us—even our most sincere efforts toward justice and peace. O God, lead us in the way of faithfulness, forgiving and transforming us in the image of Christ.

We pray for those who are victims of the world's inequalities, for the Naboths who have nowhere to turn for justice when power is exerted against them. We agonize with the victims of war and oppression. We deplore the prejudice and discrimination that prevent many of our sisters and brothers from realizing their full potential. Forgive our unknowing complicity in these evils, and grant us the courage and conviction to act where we can to bring about changes.

May all who harbor wickedness in their lives come to abhor their bloodthirsty, deceitful ways. May those of us who are pharisees be saved from ourselves. We need your love and the community you cherish for us. Hear us, we pray.　　　　　　　*Amen.*

Proper 6

Alternate

Sunday between June 12 and June 18 (if after Trinity Sunday)

2 SAMUEL 11:26–12:10, 13–15
PSALM 32

GALATIANS 2:15–21
LUKE 7:36–8:3

Out of the depth of our spirits we turn to you, O God. Hear our prayers this morning. Speak to us, that our lives may be transformed in countless ways by your loving care.

We give you thanks for the common, ordinary blessings we too often take for granted. We celebrate the sunrise, flowers, and smiles that lift our spirits. We rejoice in kind words and helpful deeds, signs of love and caring.

Even more, we rejoice in that gift of your faithfulness which enables us to know forgiveness. In Jesus Christ, we have learned most fully of your forgiveness, O God, and we are grateful. Take from us the temptations and temperament that lead us to sin. Grant us, we pray, a new and right spirit of redeemed and restored life. Help us not only to know forgiveness but also to forgive.

We pray that we may be witnesses of your love and caring. Help us, each one, to minister to others as we have been ministered to in time of need. Men and women, young and old, lay and clergy, we all have opportunities to proclaim your care by word and deed. Help us to be quick to respond when the occasion comes. Help us to be patient or courageous when appropriate, and give us wisdom to discern.

O God, be near to those who need our prayers. Give them encouragement, healing, strength, assurance. We pray for all in positions of responsibility in families, churches, and nations. Give to each one an understanding of the needs of others. Guide them in all their actions to serve those in their care.

In Jesus' name we pray.

Amen.

Bob Sandman

Proper 7

Sunday between June 19 and June 25 (if after Trinity Sunday)

1 KINGS 19:1–15a   GALATIANS 3:23–29
PSALM 42, PSALM 43   LUKE 8:26–39
OR ISAIAH 65:1–9 OR PSALM 22:19–28

O God, you are the giver of joy and courage. In this time of meditation and quiet communion, we pray that our spirits may blend with your spirit. Renew, refresh, and challenge us to attempt great things for you.

We come before you with the burdens of our lives. We have many responsibilities. We are concerned for all we know and love. There is so much in our personal lives and in the world that we cannot understand. We become confused and weary. Our strength fails us, and the journey of life is too great for us. Restore and heal us as we worship. May flowing streams of living water renew our faith and cleanse us in mind, spirit, and body.

We seek wholeness and health, not only for our own lives but also for us as a congregation and for the church universal. You make us one with you in Christ, and one with one another. You send us your light and truth, that we may know how to live according to your Word and spirit. You lift us up; you give us help and strength; you make us joyful in your presence.

Help us to remember your goodness and abiding grace as we go about our daily tasks. May we hunger and thirst for your spiritual nurture. Grant that we may find rest in your love and walk in the ways of righteousness.

We pray in the name of Jesus Christ, who has revealed you most fully to us.

Victor M. Frohne

Proper 8

Sunday between June 26 and July 2

2 KINGS 2:1–2, 6–14   GALATIANS 5:1, 13–25

PSALM 77:1–2, 11–20   LUKE 9:51–62

OR 1 KINGS 19:15–16, 19–21 OR PSALM 16

We have gathered, O God, to celebrate your wondrous works, to marvel at your redeeming activity among us. You have given us your Word, which bids us love one another. You engage us in ministry as disciples whose first priority is establishing your rule amid the competing realms of this earth. We need a double portion of your spirit to walk in the way Christ taught. *Hear*

Even as we worship you and celebrate our inheritance of faith, we recognize our infidelity. We are guilty of self-indulgence that puts our ambitions before your will. We gratify the desires of the flesh rather than seeking to grow in spirit. We deny the community into which you call us, as we bite and devour one another by our words and actions. We become controlled by our anger, jealousy, and quarreling.

O God, we have forgotten that Christ Jesus sacrificed himself to set us free. Help us to accept the gift and to refuse the yoke of bondage. Make us willing servants of the one who had nowhere to lay his head. We hear the summons, "Follow me!" and we seek to respond with joy and enthusiasm. Help us put our hands to the plow and not look back. We commit ourselves to new ways of thinking and doing, appropriate for the new millennium unfolding before us. Equip us with patience, kindness, gentleness, and self-control. Help us to be generous and faithful.

With the Holy Spirit as our guide, we go out with the confidence of prophets who parted the seas and proclaimed your Word. May Elijah's mantle fall on our shoulders as we serve in Christ's name.   *Amen.*

Proper 9

Sunday between July 3 and July 9

2 KINGS 5:1–14   GALATIANS 6:1–16

PSALM 30   LUKE 10:1–11, 16–20

OR ISAIAH 66:10–14 OR PSALM 66:1–9

Holy One, your healing presence is always moving in unlikely places. When life is raw and our desperation index gives voice to dismay, you hear our supplications. O God, be our helper. Assist us to accept the discipline of caring for our own healing by following the treatment regime of the physician and the prophet. Slow our persistent temptation to reject the healer's recommendation when our pride or our sense of self-importance is at stake. Restore in us the capacity to see you as a helper when our weeping not only clouds our eyes but also distorts our ability to see with clarity the means of healing.

With thankfulness, we recall the family, the friends, the health-care professionals, the pastor, and our colleagues who prayerfully sustained us when the foe of disease sought to turn our joy into mourning. Thank you, God, for the quiet moments in the night when the thought of you has brought our souls out of the pit of fear and despair.

Turn us away from self-pity, sustaining God. Encourage us to accept the pain that comes when we work to extend scarred muscles and bruised egos. Turn our sense of feeling sorry for ourselves into a spirit of faithful rejoicing with the steady progress toward wholeness. When we reap the rewards from doing well in aiding our healing, remind us to recall the family of faith who encouraged us to test our own work on the road to health. May the spirit of bearing one another's burdens abide with us in the days of health and joy, as you were with us in the time of hurt and fear. O God, our healer, we give thanks to you forever.   *Amen.*

Proper 10

Sunday between July 10 and July 17

AMOS 7:7–17   COLOSSIANS 1:1–14
PSALM 82   LUKE 10:25–37

OR DEUTERONOMY 30:9–14 OR PSALM 25:1–10

Eternal God, how good it is to be in your presence, to hear your Word which instructs, comforts, and empowers. Thank you for this time of quiet reflection. We celebrate your call to us, even as we ask for guidance to go with sure conviction along the paths of justice. We are grateful for those who humbly kneel to bind up the wounded and broken of our world. We celebrate those who have written your Word on their hearts and in faithfulness bear fruit for you. The many gifts you give us empower us to live life more fully than we otherwise could have imagined.

And yet, loving God, we often appear on the road to Jericho wearing the garb of the priest or the Levite, full of our own self-importance. We imagine we have a corner on your dominion. But Samaritans also walk this highway, and we are amazed how those we reject are the very ones who bind up the weak and forgotten. Forgive our arrogance and false assumptions. Purge us of twisted rhetoric that only serves our desires. In place of old lies, plant the seeds of empathy for poor and hungry children and their mothers and fathers.

O God, mother and father of this often-chaotic brood, use your wisdom and your justice to empower each of us to work for your realm and the day when all are nurtured and uplifted to become all that you intend. Remove the scales from our eyes so we may see and respond to lonely, forgotten, and suffering people. These prayers for new life we ask in Jesus' name.

Amen.

Proper 11
Sunday between July 17 and July 23

AMOS 8:1–12

PSALM 52

COLOSSIANS 1:15–28

LUKE 10:38–42

Holy God, revealed to us in Jesus of Nazareth, we are here to listen to your Word. We come to the feet of Jesus, remembering your steadfast love. As Mary received Christ's teachings, we open ourselves to all you would have us learn today. May Christ reign as head of our church, the one who reconciles us all to you and to one another.

We admit that all too often we have tried to do things our way, not Christ's way. Our words sometimes hurt others, sometimes deceive. Our actions unconsciously trample the needy and bring ruin to those who live in poverty. We aspire to riches, not righteousness; to advantages for ourselves, not allegiance to you. We are trapped by the trappings of success and no longer find in you our refuge and strength.

Thank you, God, for opening up to us fresh opportunities in spite of our faithlessness. We are not bound by our past to continue our preoccupation with things of passing worth. Your Word is still available to us, and forgiveness is offered. Your love still surrounds us when we are estranged and hostile. You call us to accept that forgiveness and love. You invite us to make your Word fully known to others. You name us among your saints and encourage us to live up to our new identity.

God of mystery and grace, how can we ask you for more? Yet we pray that you will save us, and all people, from the distractions that separate us from you. Help us to mature in Christ, with dawning wisdom and renewed hope. May we be steadfast in faith and fervent in our serving.

Amen.

Proper 11

Alternate

Sunday between July 17 and July 23

GENESIS 18:1–10*a*   COLOSSIANS 1:15–28
PSALM 15   LUKE 10:38–42

O God, immortal and invisible, Creator of the universe and Sovereign over all things, who has given us Christ as your image and presence on earth, we gather to worship and adore you today.

As in ancient times you sent messengers of hope to announce your utterances, so today you continue to reveal yourself to us in the unexpected and the amazing. How great are your gifts and your utterances, which bring hopes for our journey through life.

We rejoice in Christ, the firstborn of all creation, head of the church, who through the fullness of your love reconciles all to the Divine Self.

We thank you that we are the family of God, called to be a part of your fellowship, to live in your tent, to dwell in your presence.

You have called us to go forth blamelessly, to do what is right, to speak the truth and avoid speaking evil of others, to honor those who fear you, to take advantage of no one, and to occupy ourselves with things of lasting value.

Help us to discern what is important as we make our decisions each day.

Let us remember that you have claimed us. Though we were once estranged, now we are reconciled. As Christ inspires us, may we continue in faithfulness, stable and steadfast, not shifting in our hope of the gospel.

Even in suffering may we find a cause for rejoicing, knowing that your Word, through Christ, will reveal those hidden mysteries which can teach us wisdom as we grow to maturity in Christ.

We ask it in the name of Jesus, who gave himself for us.   *Amen.*

Proper 12

Sunday between July 24 and July 30

HOSEA 1:2–10   COLOSSIANS 2:6–19

PSALM 85   LUKE 11:1–13

OR GENESIS 18:20–32 OR PSALM 138

God of steadfast love and faithfulness, we come asking, searching, and knocking. We remember that Jesus said: "Ask and it will be given you; search and you will find; knock and the door will be opened for you." We want to believe. Yet, there are times when we have pleaded with you, God, and we have not received. We have searched for truth and meaning in many circumstances that are still a puzzle to us. It seems as if, when we knock, there is no one to open the door. Where are you, God? Are you hiding from us?

Surely there have been times when you wanted to disown us. We have not acted like your children. We have not deserved your forgiveness. We are easily captivated in the marketplace of ideas by passing fads. The lure of riches dims our sense of values. We crave recognition and power. O God, our growth has been stifled by our self-conceit. You have every reason to be angry with us. Restore us again, O God of our salvation. Revive us so your people may rejoice in you.

As we remember the prayers of Jesus, teach us to pray—not with empty words that we memorize, but with honest seeking to know you and discern your will. Reign within us and among us, that true community may be realized. We give thanks for all the gifts you have provided, with gratitude for our daily bread and all that sustains our lives. We are grateful that your offer of forgiveness is always available. We rejoice in the fresh start you extend when we forgive others. Send your Holy Spirit to us now.   *Amen.*

Proper 13

Sunday between July 31 and August 6

HOSEA 11:1–11   COLOSSIANS 3:1–11
PSALM 107:1–9, 43   LUKE 12:13–21
OR ECCLESIASTES 1:2, 12–14; 2:18–23 OR PSALM 49:1–12

How good it is to worship you, O God, and to give thanks for your steadfast love!
From our birth we have known your care. You provided for us ways to move from place
to place. You gave us the means of communicating with one another. You have embraced
us when we were hurting and redeemed us from trouble. Because of you we have known
human kindness and healing. Our hunger and thirst have been satisfied.

But we forget your goodness to us. We complain that others have more than we. It
seems that we never have quite enough. We live with an attitude of scarcity rather than
abundance. We hoard our treasures instead of sharing them. We postpone enjoyment of
your bounty.

O God, we seek the better way you have shown us in Christ Jesus. Free us from
greed, evil desire, and idolatry. Help us to rid ourselves of anger, malice, and abusive
language. Put to death all fornication, impurity, and deceit. Set our minds on Christ, that
we might be renewed, clothed with a new self, stripped of our prejudices and pettiness.

We look to your tender compassion, Holy One, not only for ourselves but also for
the whole human race. We thank you for the great variety you have created among us
while designing us for oneness and true community. We celebrate with all whom you
gather from the East and West, from the North and South. As we tremble before your
majesty, you lead us with uplifted aspirations to join you in your wonderful works. Reign
within us and establish your realm among us, we pray in Jesus' name.   *Amen.*

Proper 14

Sunday between August 7 and August 13

ISAIAH 1:1, 10–20   HEBREWS 11:1–3, 8–16

PSALM 50:1–8, 22–23   LUKE 12:32–40

OR GENESIS 15:1–6 OR PSALM 33:12–22

In the silence of the night, you come, Holy God. When we are ready for sleep, you slip into our thoughts to review the day of trouble. The pain of the day calls for a hearing in our heads and in our hearts. We remember the face of a fearful child being threatened and verbally abused in the grocery store. We recall the confused mumblings of an elderly person with a bloody lip and a broken nose in the emergency room. We were awed by the words of appreciation from families for a "thoughtful message" during a memorial service for former hospice patients. You heard the reading of their names, merciful God. Yet I continue to wonder: When will unmerited suffering and unwanted pain end?

You call us, faithful God, to travel in hope through the valley of fear, pain, and confusion. Our frail faith and our fragile hope keep us focused on a wounded world. Sustain us in the belief that a ministry of mercy is an act of obedience to your purpose. We, like Abraham and Sarah, maintain our hope because we believe you will keep your promise, God. In a time when commitments are easily made and quickly forgotten, we need the assurance of things hoped for. We need the promise of a homeland.

Thank you for the gifts that prepared us to meet the pain of others with an appropriate word or deed. Most of all, thank you for your sustaining presence, compassionate God, even when you sneak up on us in the night.   *Amen.*

Proper 15

Sunday between August 14 and August 20

ISAIAH 5:1–7   HEBREWS 11:29–12:2
PSALM 80:1–2, 8–19   LUKE 12:49–56
OR JEREMIAH 23:23–29 OR PSALM 82

God of hope-filled vision, forgive our failure to fulfill that vision. You have planted us as a vine to bring forth fruit in service to you and your people; but we have brought forth the wild fruit of selfish choices.

Prune from us the notion that your intention is for our lives to always be pleasant, and that the marks of the good life are pleasure and safety. We seek to avoid suffering, but we meet it at every turn of the road. Teach us by our suffering what you intend for us.

Save us from suffering the consequences of selfish choices, but help us to see the alternative of suffering for that which is eternal. Inspire us by the cloud of witnesses who preceded us and suffered for their faithfulness. Renew us by the vision of Jesus, the pioneer and perfecter of our faith, who for the sake of the joy that was set before him endured the cross.

By your spirit, lead us to understand our times in terms of human need. Enable us to speak the truth in love, knowing that not all will accept it. In a world which advocates unchristian values, help us to clarify choices and foster decisions for you. May we not glory in self-righteousness if our witness is a source of division. But in faithful proclamation of your will in word and deed, help us to suffer with the one who suffers with us, so that all people may be brought together, even your servant, our Savior, Jesus Christ.

Amen.

Proper 16

Sunday between August 21 and August 27

JEREMIAH 1:4–10   HEBREWS 12:18–29
PSALM 71:1–6   LUKE 13:10–17

OR ISAIAH 58:9*b*–14 OR PSALM 103:1–8

How shall we draw near if you, O God, are a consuming fire? The scorching heat is more than we can bear. We are filled with terror. How can we find you in the tempests of life when gloom surrounds us and there is no light? Are you in the wind and earthquakes and flood? Are you available when we are bent over with pain and loss and grief?

We dare to approach you today because this place of worship has been for us a safe and sacred space. It reminds us of your beauty and majesty. Here we find you a rock of refuge, a strong fortress to save us. We hear again the message that each one of us is known to you, formed by you in our mothers' wombs, consecrated from birth to a high calling as ambassadors of your Word. Your invitation to us is both frightening and compelling.

Powerful God, how can we be prophets to the nations? We scarcely know you. We have not obeyed you. We have been afraid to trust you. We have not dared to hope that your realm embraces far more than the life we know. All around us we see injustice and cruelty that deny your reign. Our doubts are often stronger than our beliefs. The realization of our unfaithfulness puts us to shame. O God, surround us with your forgiving love, that we might find wholeness, vision, and trust.

With awe and reverence, we rejoice in your promises and rededicate ourselves to a ministry of reconciliation and inclusiveness. May we respond to the voice from heaven as we go about our work in Jesus' name.   *Amen.*

Proper 17

Sunday between August 28 and September 3

JEREMIAH 2:4–13   HEBREWS 13:1–8, 15–16

PSALM 81:1, 10–16   LUKE 14:1, 7–14

OR PROVERBS 25:6–7 OR PSALM 112

God, our strength, in the security of this sacred space we find time to reflect. We recognize our subtle forgetfulness of the Holy One who breathes into us the breath of life. We also recognize our appalling acceptance of spin-doctor manipulations of truth, serving the interests of a few to the neglect of many. Gracious God, you desire truthfulness in the inner sanctuary of our lives. You have little time for self-deception or self-congratulation. Call us back to the truth proclaimed in Jesus Christ, for whom fame and fortune held no value. Call forth our courage to live faithfully and fruitfully for your purpose.

In our suspicious and untrusting days, O God, encourage us to reclaim the practice of hospitality toward those who are different from us. In a day when building more prisons is our desperate solution to the fear of violence, enable us to remember those who are confined for punishment. In a time when marriage and family take second place to desire and ambition, renew our capacity to remember the commitments we have made. Keep us from the consequences of hasty and hostile solutions. In today's atmosphere of perpetual chatter and senseless talk, strengthen our hearts and stretch our minds. Raise up leaders who will build community in which mutual love and respect can flourish.

Compassionate God, grant us a steady intention to do good, to honor all persons, and to watch over our souls so that suffering inside and outside the city gates might be reduced. May your peace complete in us your creative purposes, shaping us to your will, that we may do what is pleasing in your sight.   *Amen.*

Proper 18

Sunday between September 4 and September 10

JEREMIAH 18:1–11   PHILEMON 1–21

PSALM 139:1–6, 13–18   LUKE 14:25–33

OR DEUTERONOMY 30:15–20 OR PSALM 1

As seasons come and go, we feel your presence with us, O God. You have searched us and known us. You know when we sit down and when we rise up. You discern our every thought and are acquainted with all our ways. You have known us all our days. We were formed in your image by your own creative power. We praise you for the miracle of life, for the awesome marvel of our own bodies. Wonderful are all your works, O Creator. We are in awe when we view this amazing planet—a tiny speck in the universe over which you reign.

We marvel that you made a special visitation to this earth in Jesus of Nazareth. We have signed on as disciples, scarcely realizing the cost. Loving others as Christ did is costly business. We often shrink from taking it on. We are not eager to carry a cross. We want to avoid ridicule. We are wary lest others take advantage of us. We think of what is owed to us, not of how much we owe to you. O God, help us to listen to your voice and fit ourselves to your plan.

Thank you, God, for your willingness to reshape us as useful vessels of your love. We are eager to amend our ways. Be to us like a potter, creating beauty, molding us by the spirit of Christ. We are grateful for one another, for your work among us as we join our prayers and our labors in caring ways. We rejoice in the mutual encouragement and love that we find, serving together in Jesus' name.   *Amen.*

Proper 19

Sunday between September 11 and September 17

JEREMIAH 4:11–12, 22–28   1 TIMOTHY 1:12–27

PSALM 14   LUKE 15:1–10

Dear loving God, we come to you today conscious of our shortcomings. We realize we have not always done what we should. None of us is perfect. None of us comes close to being Christlike. We all fall short. In the complexities and heavy pressures of modern life, dear God, it is so easy to get lost. Young people are especially vulnerable. Without ample experience in living, it is difficult to evaluate circumstances accurately. Longing to show independence and strength, both youth and adults at times may misjudge. Help and guide us all.

We know that you are a God of justice and cannot condone wrongdoing. Though there are consequences, we are grateful for your mercy. We need your strength to lift us up. Please help us to trust you to bring us through the miry swamp where we stumble and struggle, trying to get ahead. Give us a longing for your presence. As in the desert one longs for flowing water, help us here to thirst for God.

We give you thanks for your mercy. Enable us in our gratefulness to be channels of mercy to others. As Christ was long-suffering, help us also to be patient with those who are driving recklessly along the highway of life. Enable us to be loving, forgiving, and teaching. Above all, help us not to return evil for evil, but to forbear, knowing that you uphold the universe.

Dear God, please hear us so that we gradually can become more like Christ and feel the kind of feelings that Christ would feel and think the kind of thoughts that Christ would think. In Christ's name, we ask.   *Amen.*

Proper 19

Alternate

Sunday between September 11 and September 17

EXODUS 32:7–14   1 TIMOTHY 1:12–17

PSALM 51:1–10   LUKE 15:1–10

Lord, have mercy upon us. Christ, have mercy upon us. Lord, have mercy upon us.

Loving God, your mercies astound us.

We wander away from you, and you seek us out.

We hide from you, and you search unceasingly to find us.

We are so small, so seemingly insignificant, and yet you know us by name.

You show us that we are infinitely precious.

How great is your faithfulness, a source of everlasting wonder.

Hear us now as we come to you again, with repentant hearts, seeking to be restored.

We have broken your covenant of trust.

You gave us your commandments, and we turned our backs upon them,

    seeking an easier way.

You gave us your Child, Jesus, and we insulted and rejected him.

You called us to love our neighbors, and we said that was impossible.

In betraying you, we have betrayed ourselves.

But to those whose sin is greatest, your mercies abound.

Your sentence of judgment is not death, but new life.

You come to heal us, to grant us wisdom, to bring hope for change.

We are not lost.

Remember our good deeds and transform us.

For your mercy is from everlasting to everlasting.

Amen.

Julie Ruth Harley

Proper 20

Sunday between September 18 and September 24

JEREMIAH 8:18–9:1   1 TIMOTHY 2:1–7

PSALM 79:1–9   LUKE 16:1–13

OR AMOS 8:4–7 OR PSALM 113

One and only God, whom we glimpse in the Scriptures and encounter in Jesus Christ, we bring our supplications, intercessions, and thanksgiving, wanting to lead a quiet and peaceable life in all godliness and dignity. We want to be faithful in all things, for we recognize you as the creator and ruler of all worlds. All that we enjoy as a nation and as individuals is an inheritance from you, to be treasured and passed on, enriched by our efforts and our caring.

We confess, to our dismay, that we have taken you for granted, God. We have pretended that all we have is the result of our own efforts. We invest so much of ourselves in the things we have and those to which we aspire that there is no time for you in our busy schedules. Our possessions possess us and become our idols. Our houses of worship are defiled, not by vandals, but by our hypocrisy. We cry to you to save us, but we are not willing to give up control. We want health while retaining some of our sinful ways. Help us, O God of our salvation; deliver us and forgive our sins, for your name's sake.

O Great Physician, whose healing waters are meant for all people, we give thanks that you enlist us in your service. We are grateful for Jesus Christ, the great mediator, who set the example for us. May we be heralds and apostles, reaching out in faith and truth to friends, neighbors, and enemies alike, in Christ's name.   *Amen.*

Proper 21

Sunday between September 25 and October 1

JEREMIAH 32:1–3*a*, 6–15   1 TIMOTHY 6:6–19

PSALM 91:1–6, 14–16   LUKE 16:19–31

OR AMOS 6:1*a*, 4–7 OR PSALM 146

Our refuge and our fortress, O God, in whom we trust, we seek to dwell in the shelter of your wings. Amid the terrors of the night and the bullets that fly by day, we turn to you. When illness strikes or our security is threatened, we cry out for your protection.

We confess that we are less conscious of your presence when all is going well. By wanting to be rich, we fall into temptation. We become entrapped by many senseless and harmful desires. We begin to love money more than people. Faith becomes a secondary compartment instead of the heart of life. Your commandments become mere suggestions. Your will is no longer our way.

How long has it been since we really noticed those who are poor, hungry, or homeless?—sincerely recognized them as brothers and sisters in Christ? Oh, we have our feeding programs, and our overnight shelters. We fill up our mitten trees and charity boxes at Christmastime. But the chasm between rich and poor deepens, and by our silence we consent. We recognize our guilt, even as we profit from the sweat of others.

Still you call us to pursue righteousness. You invite us to a godliness we have not yet experienced. You see in us the potential for faith, love, endurance, and gentleness. You remind us of our baptism and of the vows we have professed. You recall us to good works and generous sharing as eager disciples of Jesus. You set our priorities straight and renew our hopes. Thank you for helping us take hold of life that really is life! *Amen.*

Proper 22

Sunday between October 2 and October 8

LAMENTATIONS 1:1–6   2 TIMOTHY 1:1–14

PSALM 137   LUKE 17:5–10

OR HABAKKUK 1:1–4; 2:1–4 OR PSALM 37:1–9

Holy God, we remember, and we weep. We remember our mothers and fathers, our grandparents in the faith. We recall times when our faith was strong, when our churches were centers of community. Our tears flow with a sense of loss. We are not happy with what we have become: consumers of religion, not disciples of Jesus; captive to the latest fads, not innovators with a treasure to share.

We pray with the apostles, "Increase our faith!" But we are not daring enough to nourish the mustard seed. For faith, we know, is not an intellectual exercise but a matter of trust, and, God, we have forgotten how to trust. We have grave reservations about spiritual matters—about factors we cannot measure and a God we cannot see. So we pray without expectancy and we live without an eternal reference point. How can we sing the songs of faith in a secular society?

Amazing God, you come to us in spite of our laments, despite our cowardice, in the midst of our doubts. You rekindle your gifts within us. Thank you for a spirit of power and of love and of self-discipline. Thank you for abolishing death and granting us new life. Thank you for enlisting us as servants among your lost children, as teachers of your Word, as apostles of light. You have offered us the help of the Holy Spirit. You have promised us your grace to carry us beyond the limits of our own works. O God, as we accept our holy calling, we are filled with joy. Receive now our renewed commitment.

Amen.

Proper 23

Sunday between October 9 and October 15

JEREMIAH 29:1, 4–7   2 TIMOTHY 2:8–15

PSALM 66:1–12   LUKE 17:11–19

OR 2 KINGS 5:1–3, 7–15c OR PSALM 111

We gather our bodies, our minds, and our hearts in your presence, Holy God, seeking as a community to know your grace and to share with you our truest selves. You have sent us forth as your people, called to minister, to proclaim your message and live by its truth. Often we find ourselves to be strangers, striving for compassion and truth in a world that little values them. Yet it is for this world that we pray, O God—for its welfare is our welfare; its future is our future.

We pray for those swallowed up by violence, poverty, or persecution, that they might have reason to hope again. We pray for those forgotten in institutions and prisons and refugee camps, that they might be assured that you—and we—care about them. We pray for those seeking healing and wholeness [name congregants in need], and for the very planet by which you sustain us, that they might receive what they need to be all you intend for them.

Gracious God of love, we have come as individuals and as a people through fires and floods and sufferings that only you know, yet you have always brought us through to a spacious place. Our needs are satisfied, our safety assured in your embrace. Keep us persistent in living the gospel, whether in hardship or ease, as witnesses of a saving grace in this needy, needy world. In the name of Christ we pray. *Amen.*

Jennifer Amy-Dressler

Proper 24

Sunday between October 16 and October 22

JEREMIAH 31:27–34   2 TIMOTHY 3:14–4:5

PSALM 119:97–104   LUKE 18:1–8

OR GENESIS 32:22–31 OR PSALM 121

O God beyond our knowing, we celebrate the glimpses of yourself, revealed in the Scriptures. You have inspired countless writers to witness to your work among us. Their words have instructed us in the faith of Jesus Christ. They challenge and correct us and equip us for every good work. Your Word, through them, guides our meditation, deepens our understanding, and draws us into covenant relationship with you.

Like the Hebrew people before us, we have often forgotten the covenant. We have broken our promise to be your people guided by your commandments and the example of Jesus. We have accumulated teachers to suit our own desires. Our itching ears have turned away from your truth to follow the heralds of financial success and social popularity. As we have prospered, it has become more difficult to identify with those who are poor. Enjoying the benefits of education, being part of the "in" majorities, and having favorable connections, we have given little notice to injustice. O God, forgive our ignorance, disinterest, and avoidance of those whose desperate plight makes us uncomfortable.

We are thankful for the new covenant you offer us in Jesus Christ. The teachings of Jesus are written on our hearts. Your way of love, embodied in Jesus, is a persuasive influence on our lives. You have put your law within us, and we cannot forget it even when we try to evade it. How amazing that you have given us this way of knowing you!

May we fulfill our ministry to and with all for whom you ask us to pray. Equip us as evangelists who teach with patience and encourage with enthusiasm, in Christ's name.

Amen.

Proper 25

Sunday between October 23 and October 29

JOEL 2:23–32   2 TIMOTHY 4:6–8, 16–18
PSALM 65   LUKE 18:9–14
OR JEREMIAH 14:7–10, 19–22 OR PSALM 84:1–7

Awesome God, we are glad as we rejoice at the gateways of the morning. We have awakened once more to the wonders of mountains and seas and lands overflowing with abundant harvests. You crown this year with bounty for all to enjoy.

Yet even when we have so much, most of us are not satisfied. Deliver us, O God, from the whiners and blamers of this age. From centers of power to back alleys of poverty, people proclaim that others are at fault for their troubles. We join in twisted tales of half-truths to justify our complaints. We cynically cut others down to sustain our petty conceits. Our deeds of iniquity overwhelm us.

Holy God, open our eyes to how you see us. Bring us face to face with the honest truth of our ingratitude in a land of plenty. Do we seem to you like swarming locusts, cutting and destroying the gifts of life? We hear your gentle rebuke, knowing that we often deserve a harsher judgment. Deliver us from the destructive power of our self-justifying attitude.

Thank you, O God, for your mercy toward sinners. We are amazed and humbled when we stand before you, aware of who you are, and who we are. We are awed at the realization that you answer our prayers. You pour out your spirit on all flesh, that we may dream and prophesy and catch a vision of life as you intend. You equip us to finish the race and keep the faith. Your acceptance of us gives us strength and courage to follow Christ, in whose name we pray.

Amen.

Proper 26

Sunday between October 30 and November 5

HABAKKUK 1:1–4, 2:1–4   2 THESSALONIANS 1:1–4, 11–12

PSALM 119:137–144   LUKE 19:1–10

OR ISAIAH 1:10–18 OR PSALM 32:1–7

We praise you, O God, that you are a God of righteousness and mercy, and that we may come to you with our complaints as well as thanksgivings.

Like psalmists and prophets of old, there are times when we cry out in anger and anguish against the evil so prevalent around us. Wherever we look are oppression, strife, contention, abuse, disrespect for life and property. Laws are broken and not enforced; justice often seems perverted. The proud and arrogant trust in themselves; they appear to outnumber the righteous. We wonder and ask, "How long, O God, will you tolerate injustice and wrongdoing? How long must we wait for you to act and restore justice?"

Speak to us, we humbly ask, in ways that are plain and clear for everyone to see your vision of shalom—that what it speaks of is true! Help us to trust in your precepts, for they are best; they bring life and strength in the midst of difficulty.

Christ Jesus, come to us with your grace as you came to Zacchaeus. When you came to him, he responded in faith, and salvation came to his house. When he received your grace and love, he became a new creature—showing justice and kindness, returning fraudulent profits, living righteously, rejoicing in his newfound freedom. So may it be with us, that we, too, may extend righteousness, mercy, and kindness to others.

Hear us as we pray for one another to be made worthy of your call, to glorify you, and to be steadfast unto you alone. We ask in Jesus' name.   *Amen.*

All Saints' Day

DANIEL 7:1–3, 15–18   EPHESIANS 1:11–23

PSALM 149   LUKE 6:20–31

Holy and wonderful God, we, your people, are humbled by so grand an inheritance as you offer us. Our immediate response is to move away from daily tasks and duties in order to pause and thank you. As our spirits mingle with your spirit in these moments of worship, we are filled with awe and gratitude. We pray that our simple and sincere thanksgivings might be pleasing to you.

Jesus has called us to "remember" in so many ways, yet, full of ourselves, we forget the lessons of the yesterdays and fail to heed Christ's example and the example of saints of the past. In so doing, we have also failed to recognize other "saints" all around us: condemning the poor, ignoring the hungry, bypassing those who mourn, and reviling those who stand up for justice. God, forgive us as we have taken much and given little. Help us to be with the poor, the hungry, the grieving, and the persecuted, just as you have been with us in our poverty, our hunger, our grief, and our times of persecution.

"For all the saints who from their labors rest,"* we offer up an "Alleluia!" The good faith and simple courage of these people give evidence to us that even in the midst of monstrous moments you will not abandon us, you will be our strong salvation if we but believe! Thank you, O God, for the victories you've given your saints of bygone days. Thank you, God, for the victories, great and small, that are yet to come. In surrendering our lives to you, we can turn the other cheek, we can be truly generous to all we meet.

Amen.

*William W. How, 1864

Proper 27

Sunday between November 6 and November 12

HAGGAI 1:15*b*–2:9

PSALM 145:1–5, 17–21

2 THESSALONIANS 2:1–5, 13–17

LUKE 20:27–38

OR JOB 19:23–27*a* OR PSALM 17:1–9

Mighty God, glorious in your splendor and majestic in all your works, we praise and bless your name. Our ancestors have heard your promises and witnessed to their fulfillments. They found you to be just in all your ways and kind in all your doing. You answered their cries, watched over them, and poured out your love on all who were open to receive it.

But we have felt the earth shake. The truth we embraced has been challenged. The goodness we saw in one another has been betrayed. Traditions we honored have crumbled all around us. Your way is not clear to us. We have stumbled and fallen, fearing that we are all alone. We have become creatures of death, not children of the resurrection. Reach out to forgive and heal us, we pray.

We thank you for the brothers and sisters who journey with us through life. We want to join with them in proclaiming the good news of salvation. How glad we are for the assurance that Christ will comfort our hearts and strengthen us in every good work and word! We are grateful that you call us to fullness of life, that you reveal grace and joy and meaning.

Our prayers today embrace your children who live in constant danger. May all who fear find courage, those whose losses overwhelm know your steadfast love, and all who exist in the grip of hatred and violence be turned away from terror. Grant endurance in the face of adversity. We pray that each of us may recommit ourselves to faithful service, showing forth the fruits of salvation in our words and actions. *Amen.*

Proper 28

Sunday between November 13 and November 19

ISAIAH 65:17–25

ISAIAH 12

2 THESSALONIANS 3:6–13

LUKE 21:5–19

God of truth, we hear your promise of new heavens and a new earth. We long for fulfillment of that dream. We live in a time of small talk. Airways are filled with the chatter of busybodies. The titillating verbiage of talk show hosts feeds our sordid curiosity. We clamor for intimate details of troubled lives while, in our own households, we seldom converse on subjects that matter. As we sit before the TV, grunting and groaning to one another, we sometimes feel like strangers in our own homes.

Dear God, save us from the terrifying inability to face one another. We are hurt and destroyed within as our souls slowly starve to death before the talking heads on the tube. Move us off our couches into community. Be our strength and our might as we learn to carry on hopeful conversation with two or three gathered in your name. Open our ears to hear: "Surely God is our salvation. We will trust and not be afraid."

Amid the storms of life, we need the healing power of compassionate conversation. Grant us the words and wisdom for encouraging dialogue. May joy spring forth from the refreshing wells of shared stories. Link our lives with the work and words of Jesus, that we might endure in troubled times. Move us to songs of praise as we realize how you have gifted us with mind, heart, and memory. We give thanks, Holy One, that you have blessed us with the gift of speech. Grant courage to proclaim your presence within our families, in conversation with friends, in our work and play. May conversation become a well of salvation among us.

Amen.

Alternate

Sunday between November 13 and November 19

MALACHI 4:1–2*a*   2 THESSALONIANS 3:6–13
PSALM 98   LUKE 21:5–19

You are coming, God! The day of judgment is certain. Yet the psalmist assures us that you are honest and fair. You have the power to save and to bring justice.

We see signs of your love all around us, and we await with expectant hearts Christ's return to our earth. We confess that we have only believed half-heartedly in your promises contained in the Scriptures. We confess that we have believed in the parts of the Bible that have suited us, while we have ignored the difficult passages that speak of end times and cataclysmic events. Any way we look at it, someday we will see you face to face, either on earth or in heaven. Sometimes this frightens us, but at other times we want to clap and sing and dance for joy.

Lead us, God. Speak to us as a people and as the church, that we might be faithful to you until the end. Don't let our faith in you be something we observe only on Sunday, but make us fierce doers of the gospel throughout the week and in every area of our lives. Help us to discern your will and your reign in these difficult days. Help us to be truly thankful people, to see your hand working in our days and in our world.

May we participate in your coming realm, in our daily decisions, as well as observing your love and power working in our nation and in the struggles of people around the world to be free and to know you. We commit this prayer in the name of the Coming One—Jesus Christ.   *Amen.*

Proper 29 (Reign of Christ)

Sunday between November 20 and November 26

JEREMIAH 23:1–6   COLOSSIANS 1:11–20
LUKE 1:68–79   LUKE 23:33–43

OR JEREMIAH 23:1–6 OR PSALM 46

Blessed Redeemer of your people, we praise you for the mercy shown to our ancestors. When they were scattered, you gathered them to yourself. When they were fearful, you gave them courage. When they were in grave danger, you rescued them from their enemies. You guided them in the way of peace. Their sins were forgiven, and they welcomed the healing of your saving grace. Bring stillness to us here, that we, too, might know that you are God.

O God, we are troubled by all the changes around us. We feel that we cannot trust one another. In our differences, we see threat rather than opportunity to expand our understanding. All around us we observe crumbling relationships, job insecurity, families scattered, and hopes denied. Shed your light on us, we pray. We need the guidance and courage which our forebears found in you. Heal our brokenness. Forgive our sin.

Thank you, gracious God, for inviting us into the company of saints where Christ reigns. We are discovering in the practice of self-giving love a power that transcends scoffing, mocking, and derision. Where Christ is truly the head of the church, there is reconciliation and peacemaking in spite of differences. We are grateful that in Christ all things hold together.

We have good news to share with the world. Help us to be builders of genuine community, that others might be drawn toward the wholeness you offer. Guide our outreach and service so we may offer genuine help to meet the needs of people who live around us as well as linking hands with others around the whole earth.

Amen.

Thanksgiving Day

DEUTERONOMY 26:1–11
PSALM 100

PHILIPPIANS 4:4–9
JOHN 6:25–35

O God, as we celebrate this Thanksgiving Day, forgive us if we find it hard to be thankful. Should we be thankful that we will soon have a wonderful thanksgiving dinner while others starve? Should we be thankful for good health when others are sick, or grateful for jobs when others are out of work? Can we be grateful that though we live in an imperfect world, in the midst of too much and too little, there still can be love? In a world where some weep and others laugh and injustice reigns, can we still have faith and hope?

Yes, God, we not only can but we must be thankful for the gifts of life which you have bestowed on us all. Most especially we are grateful for the life of Jesus. Through Christ we can live above and beyond our successes and failures in moments filled with eternity. Help us to look beyond the perishable things of daily living to those which are everlasting, putting our trust and hope in Christ alone.

In gratitude may we bring the first sample of our harvest to you, acknowledging that, in mysterious ways, you have brought us all to this bountiful land. Hear our prayers for [name petitions].

O God of mercy, as we celebrate this day of thanksgiving, make us aware of all of the blessings that make life beautiful and of the resources of your love and strength that enable us to cope with difficult days. Minister to our needs and make us worthy of your love. Let us sing and shout with joy that we are your people and that you are our shepherd.

Glory be to you, O God! Alleluia, alleluia, alleluia!

Thanksgiving Day

DEUTERONOMY 26:1–11
PSALM 100

PHILIPPIANS 4:4–9
JOHN 6:25–35

God of steadfast love and faithfulness, we rejoice on this day of thanksgiving. It is not just the abundance we enjoy that brings us to these moments of gratitude. Much more, it is the dawning awareness of your guiding presence throughout our lives that moves us to celebrate.

We are your people, the sheep of your pasture. You were with us at our birth. You surrounded us with love as we grew. Your help was ever near amidst our struggles. Indeed, we have found that you dwell within us and among us. Your energy embraces the whole universe, yet is always available, near at hand. We give thanks and bless your name. Hear the joyful noise we make as we sing your praise.

Lead us to meditate on what is true, honorable, and just. May our thanksgiving center not so much on things as on relationships. Lift our focus beyond family and close friends to include the wanderer who has not yet found a home, the child who has never enjoyed a decent meal, the suffering outcast who has no physician. How shall we carry out your works, O God, when the needs are so great?

Today, as we partake of earthly food, may we also feast on the true bread from heaven which gives life to the world. Let the bread of life fill our hunger for meaning and quench our thirst for purposefulness. Purify our thoughts and actions, that we might desire above all else to please you. As we present to you the first fruits of our labors, may we also express in all we do the excellence that is possible when we walk in the footsteps of Christ.

Amen.

Reflections

Reflections

Index of Scripture Readings

Key: * = passages not used in preparing prayers for this volume.
      Italic = alternate readings during the season after Pentecost.

Hebrew Scriptures

JOB

PSALMS

Reflections

Reflections

Reflections